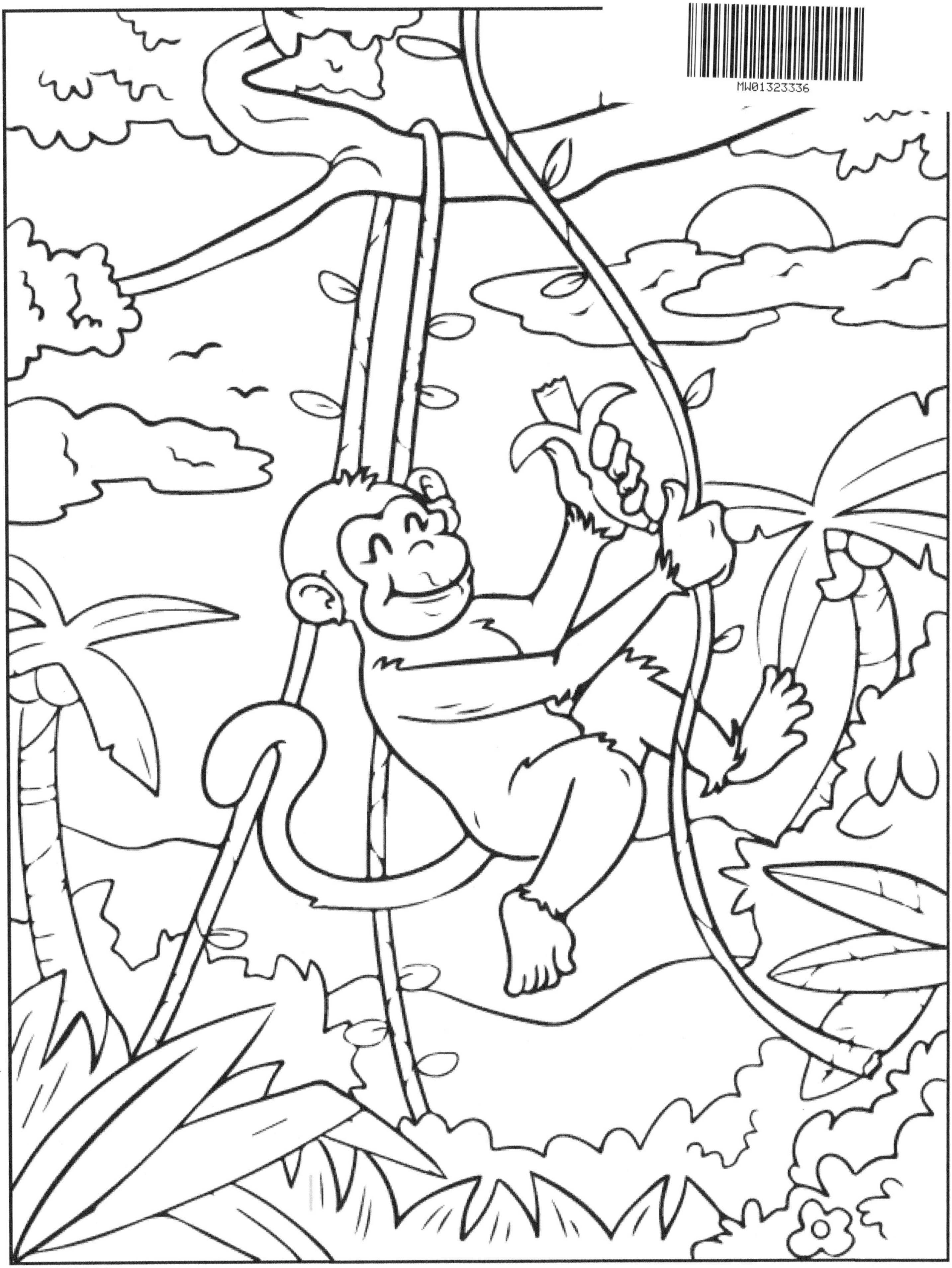

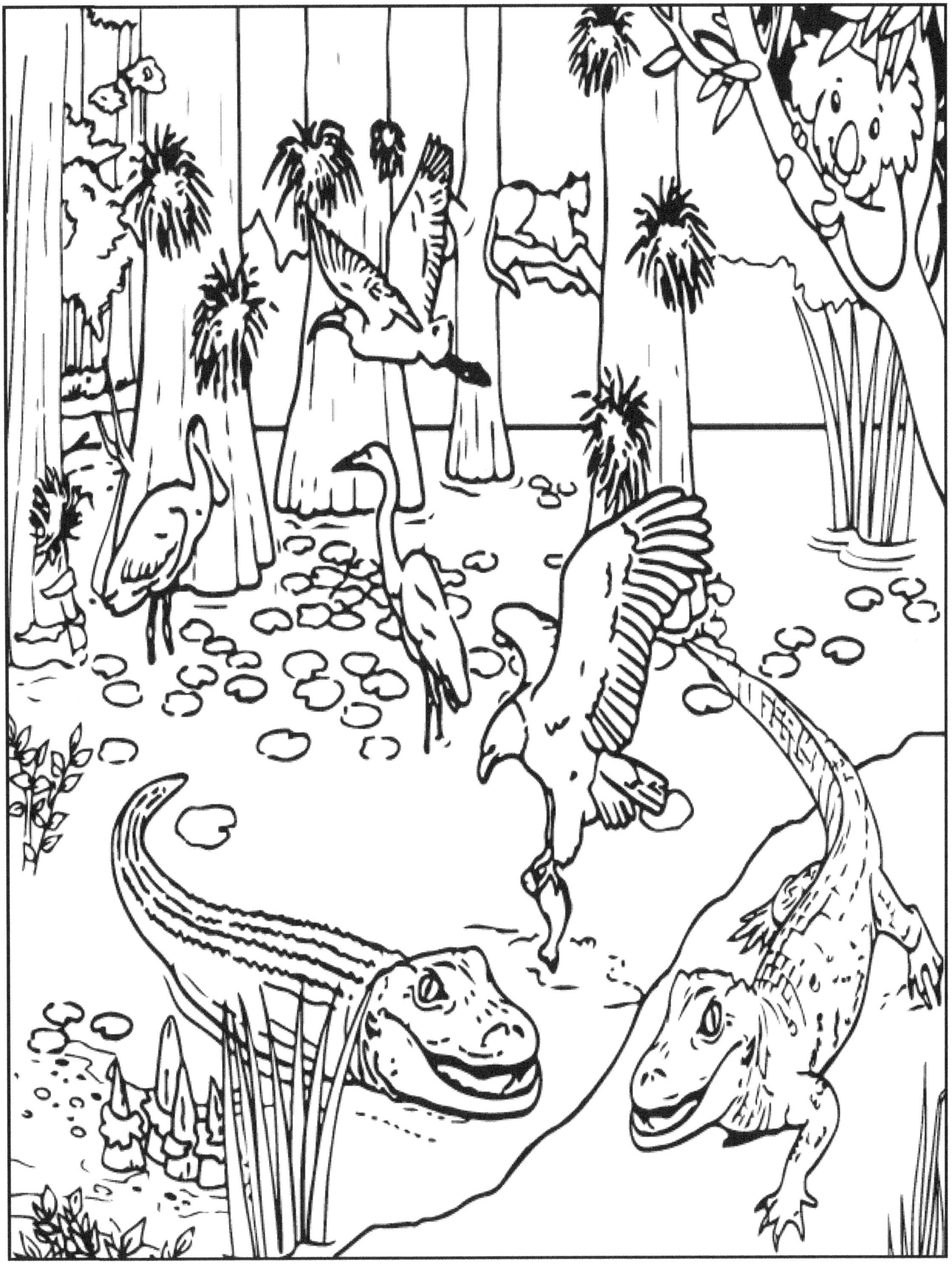

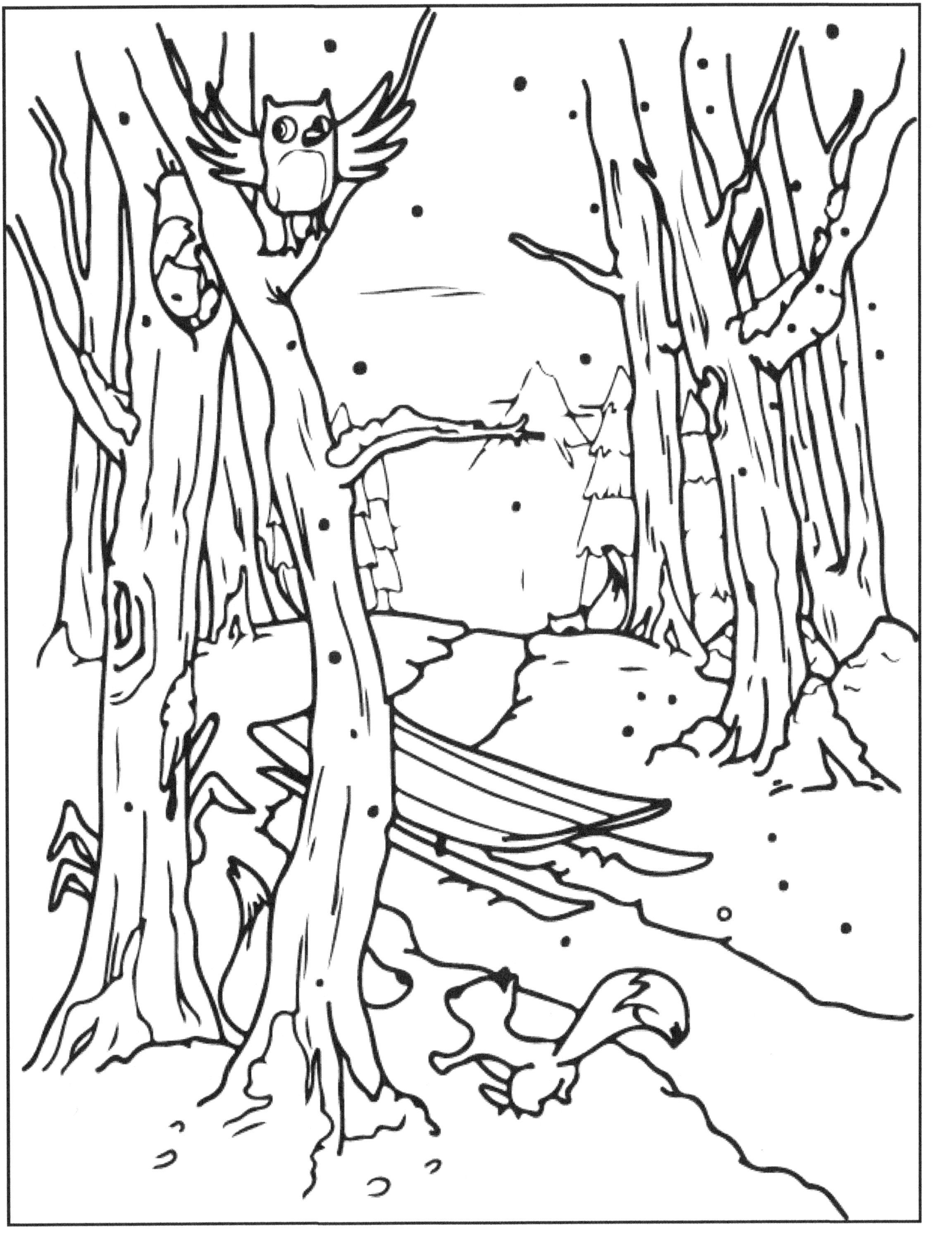

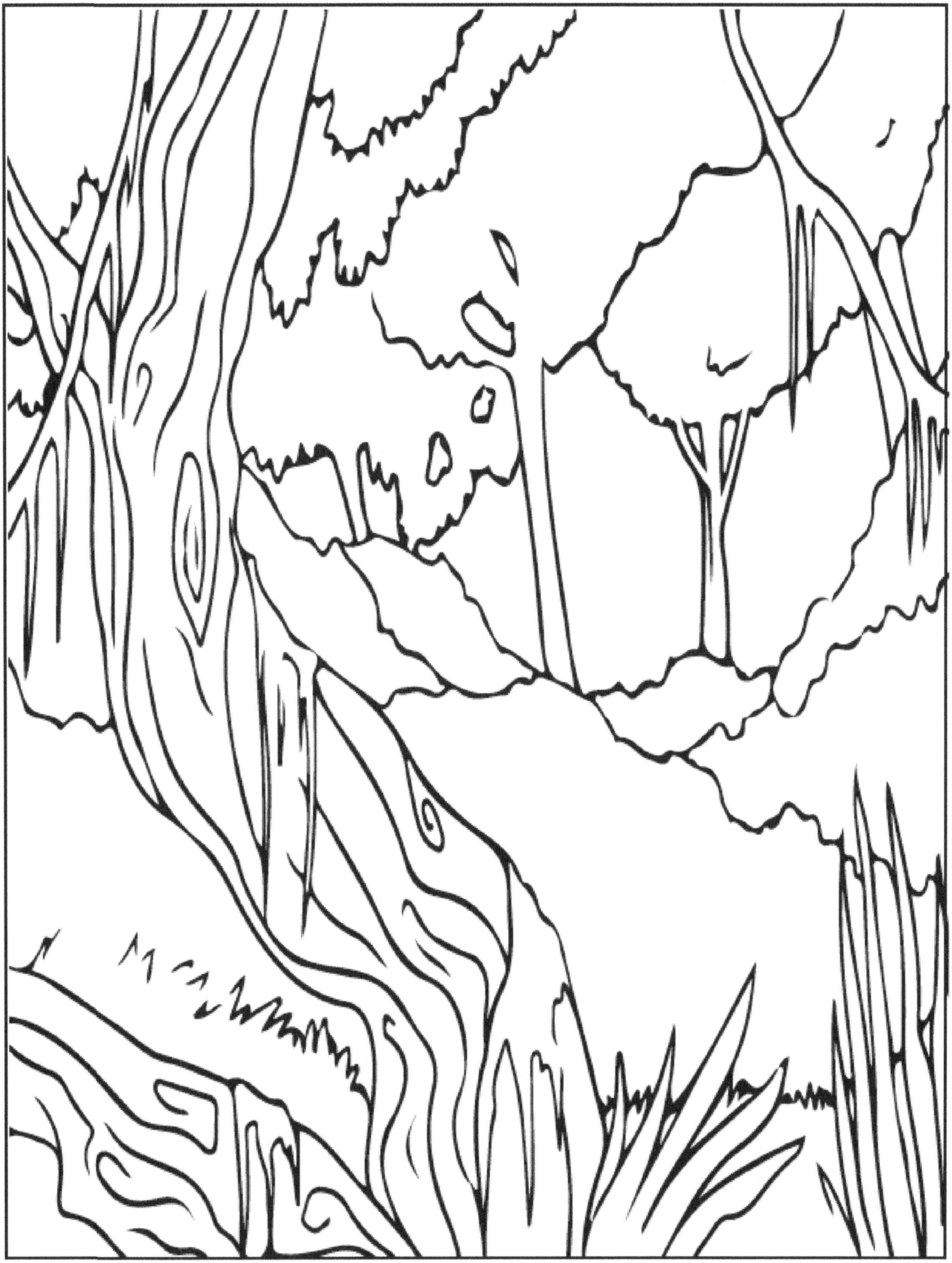

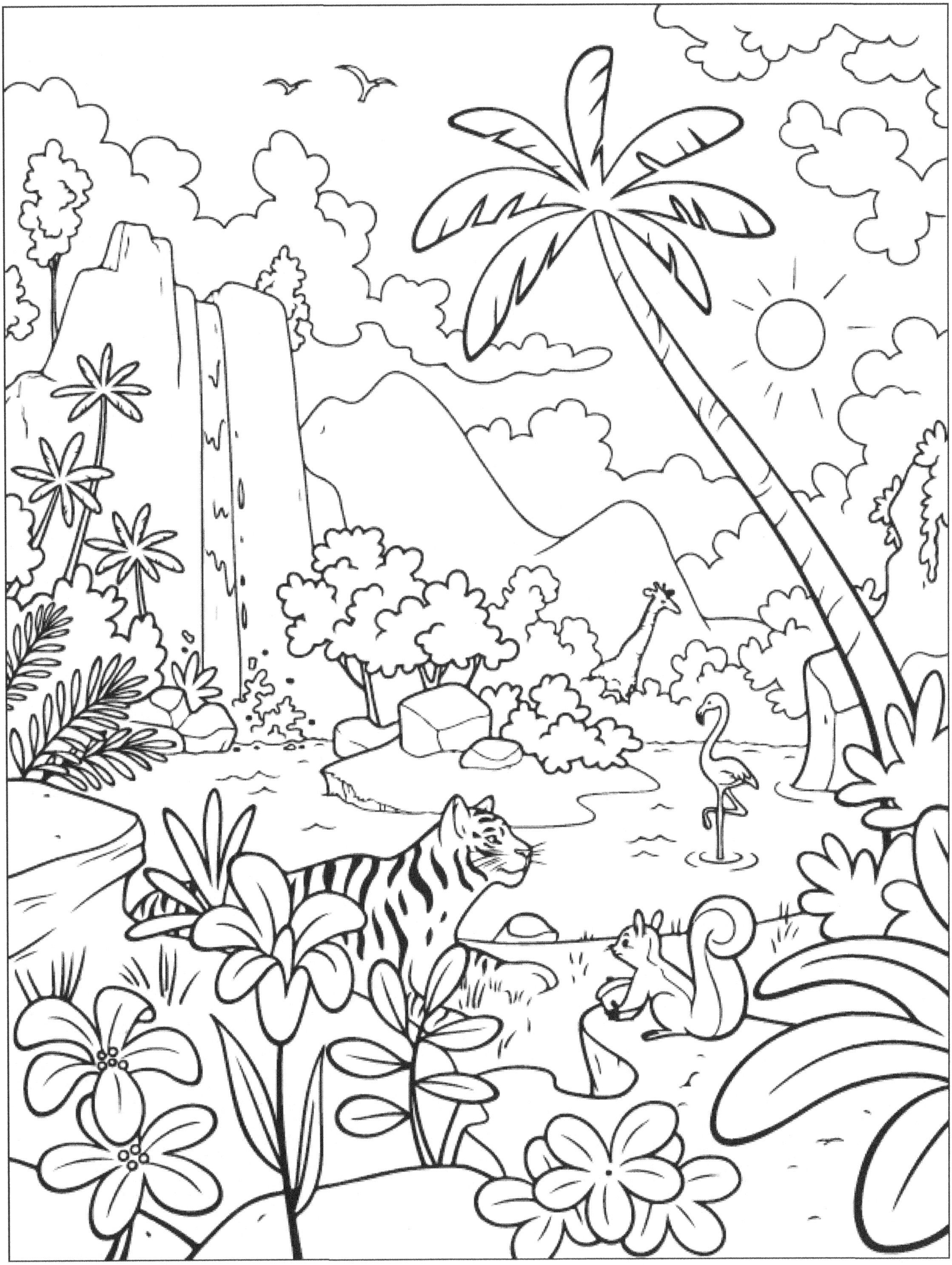

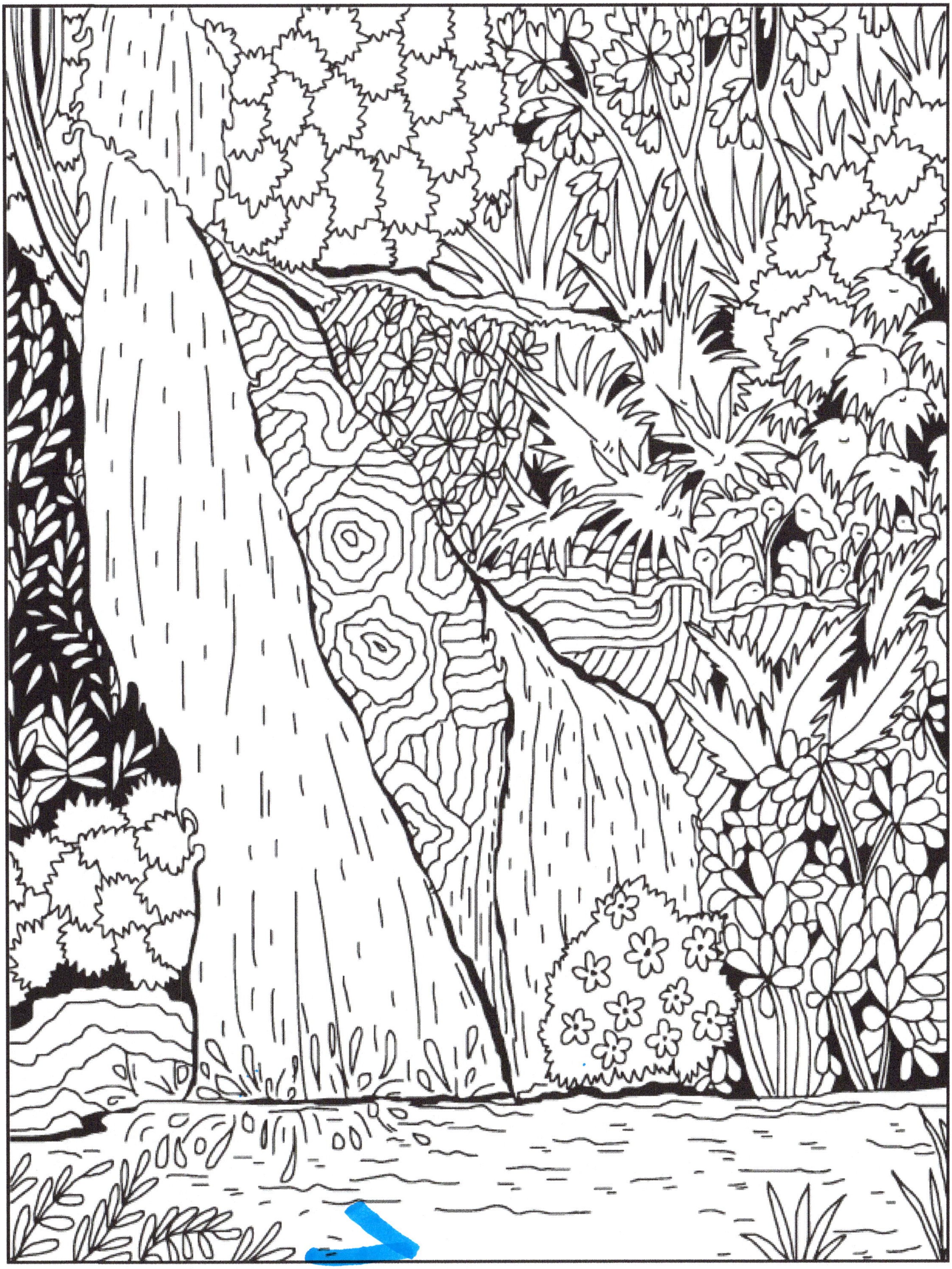

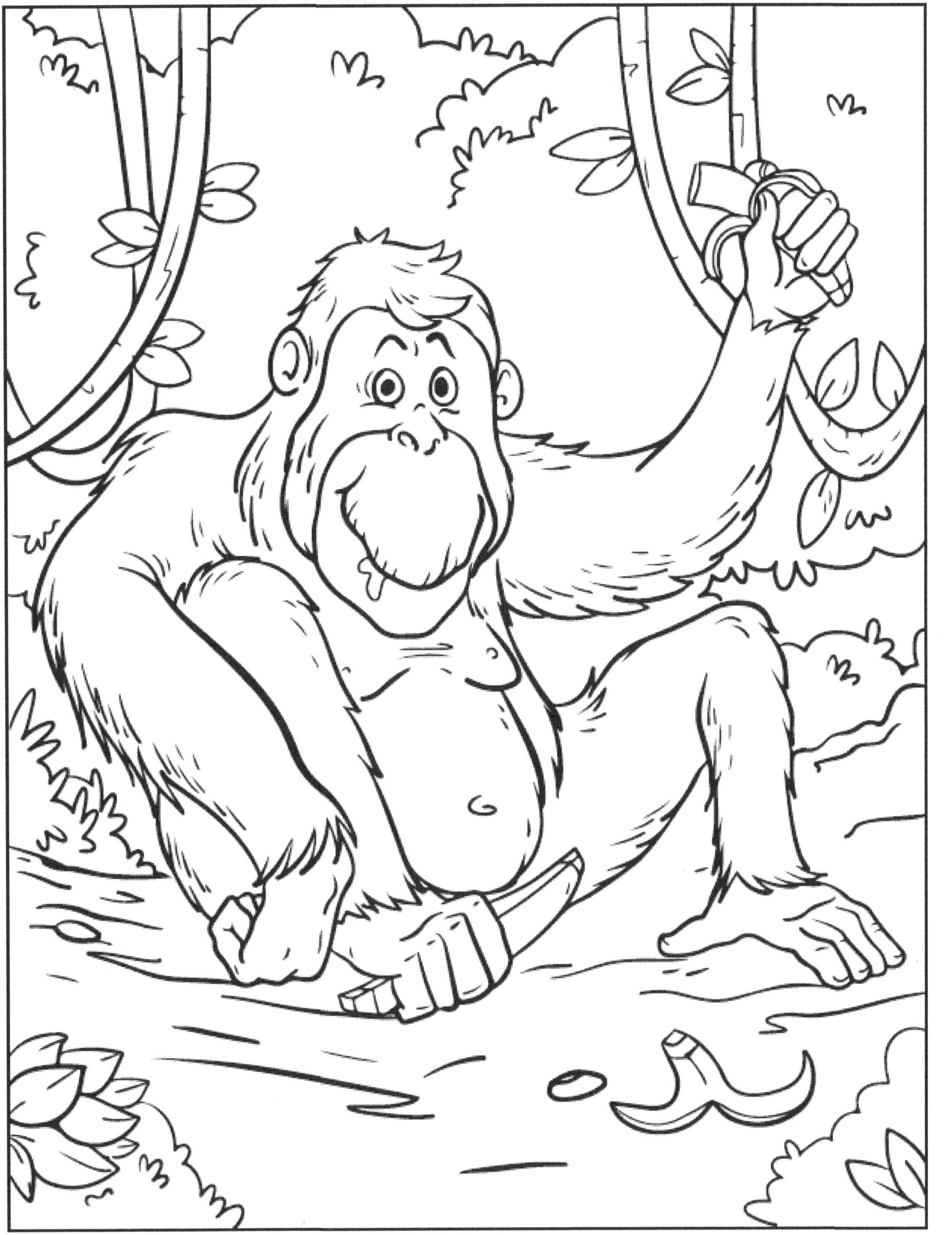

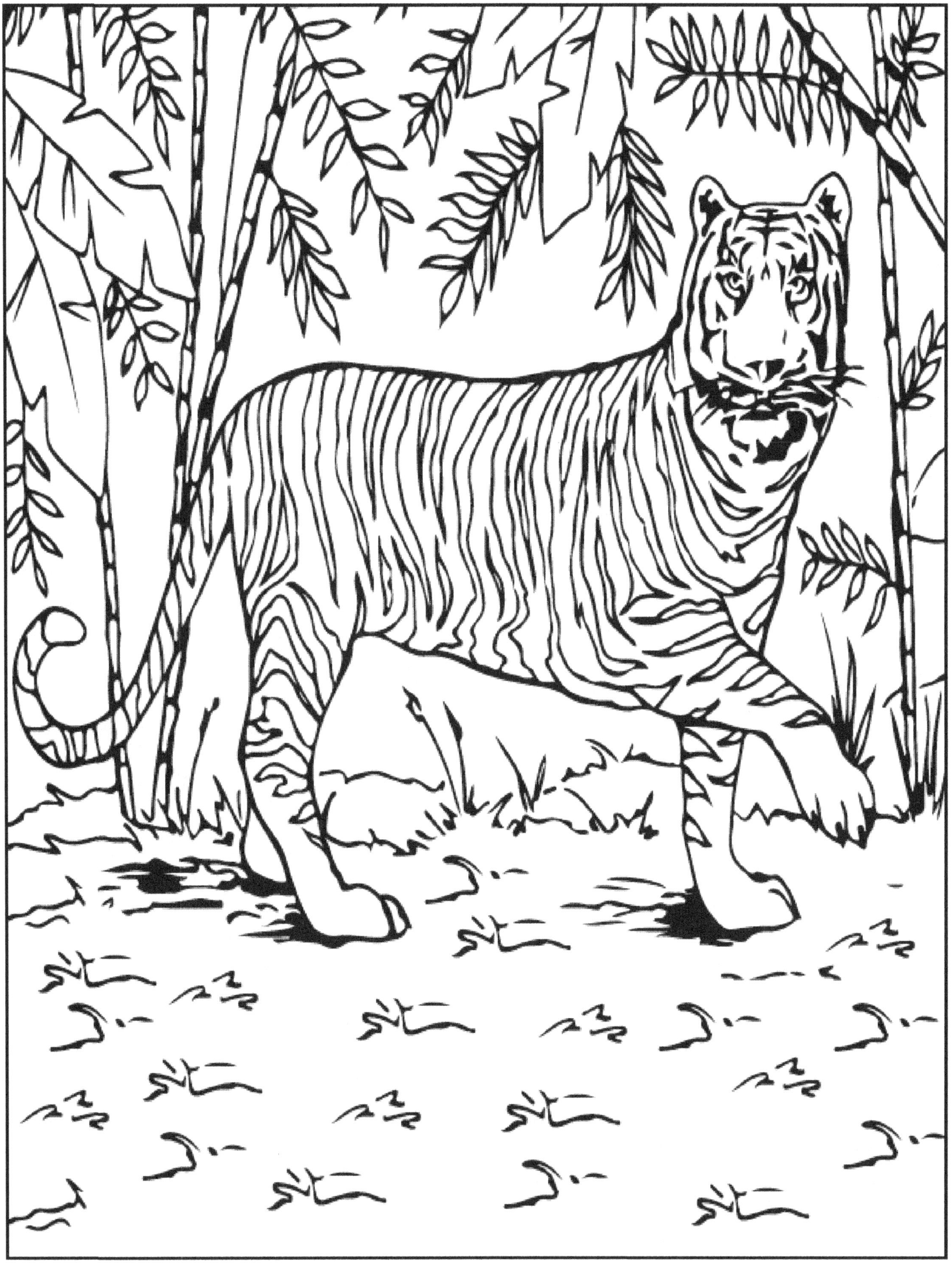

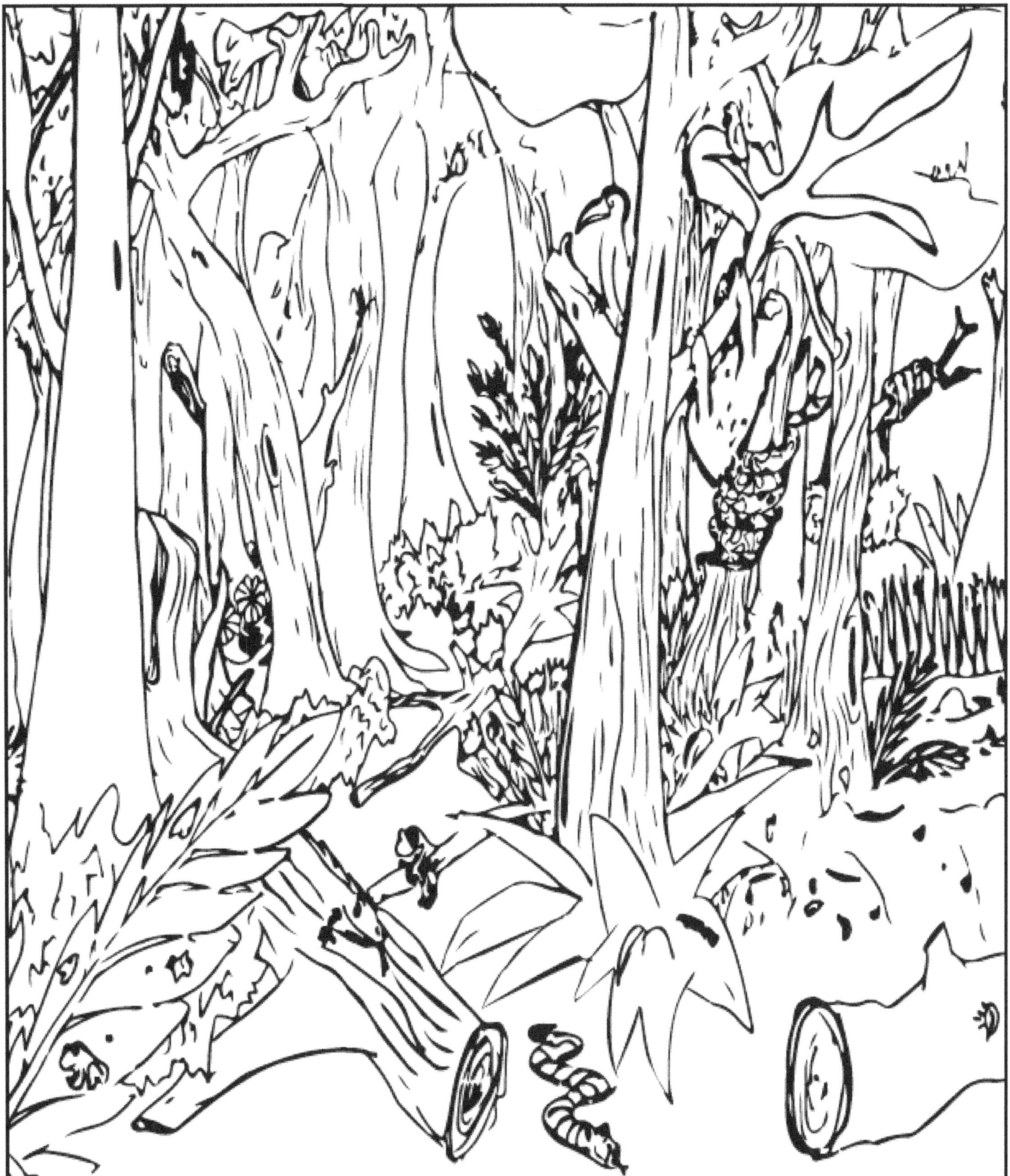

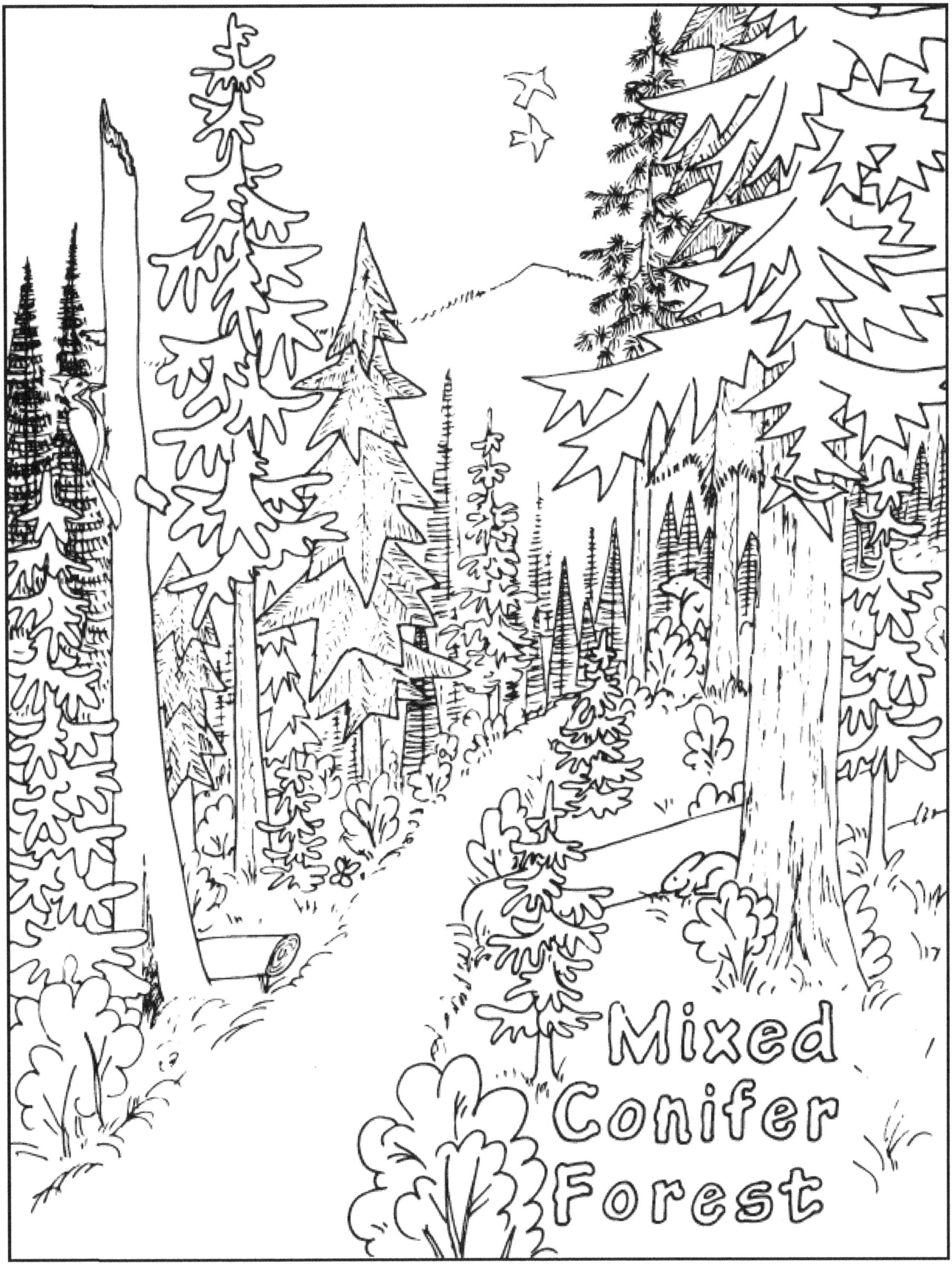
Mixed
Conifer
Forest

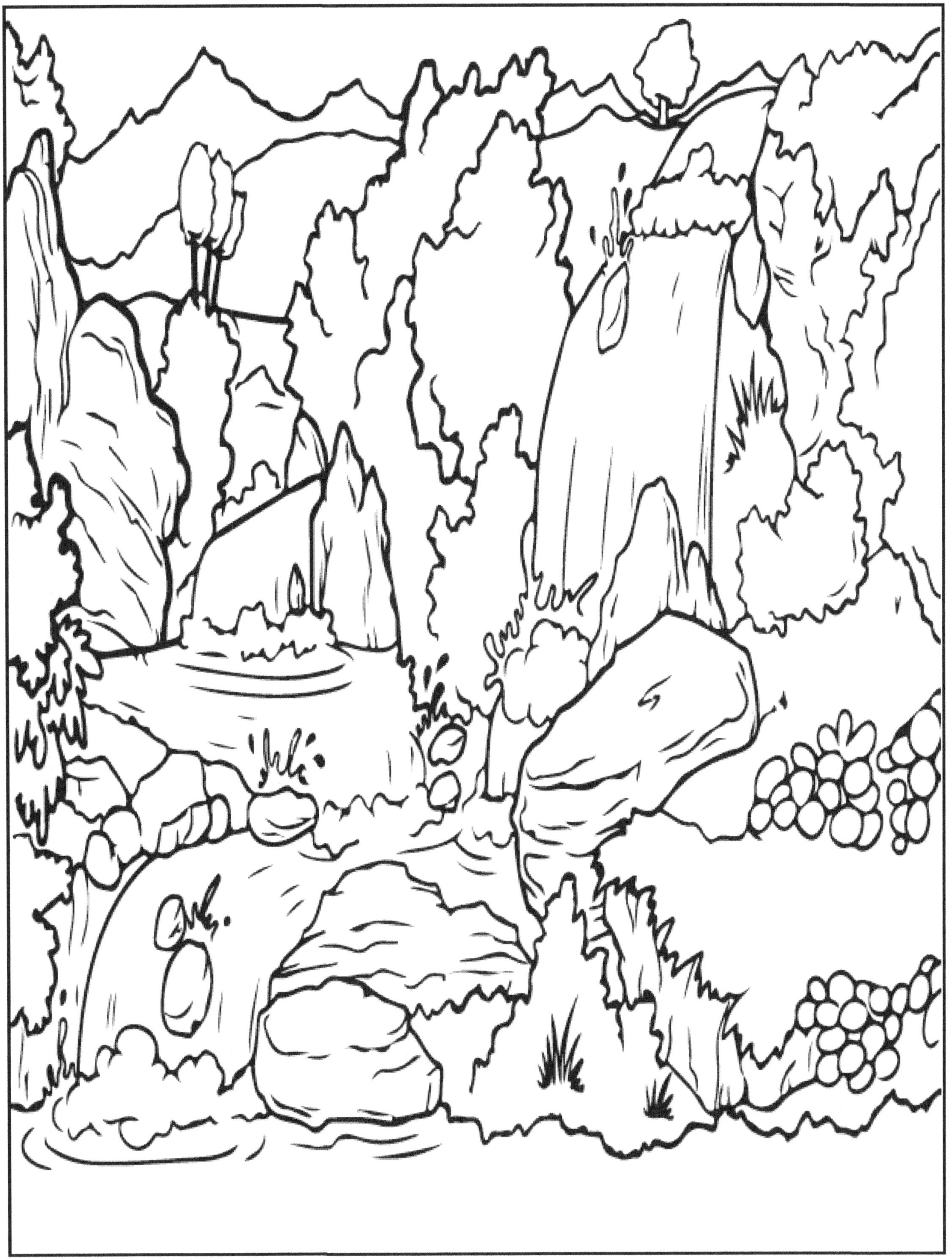

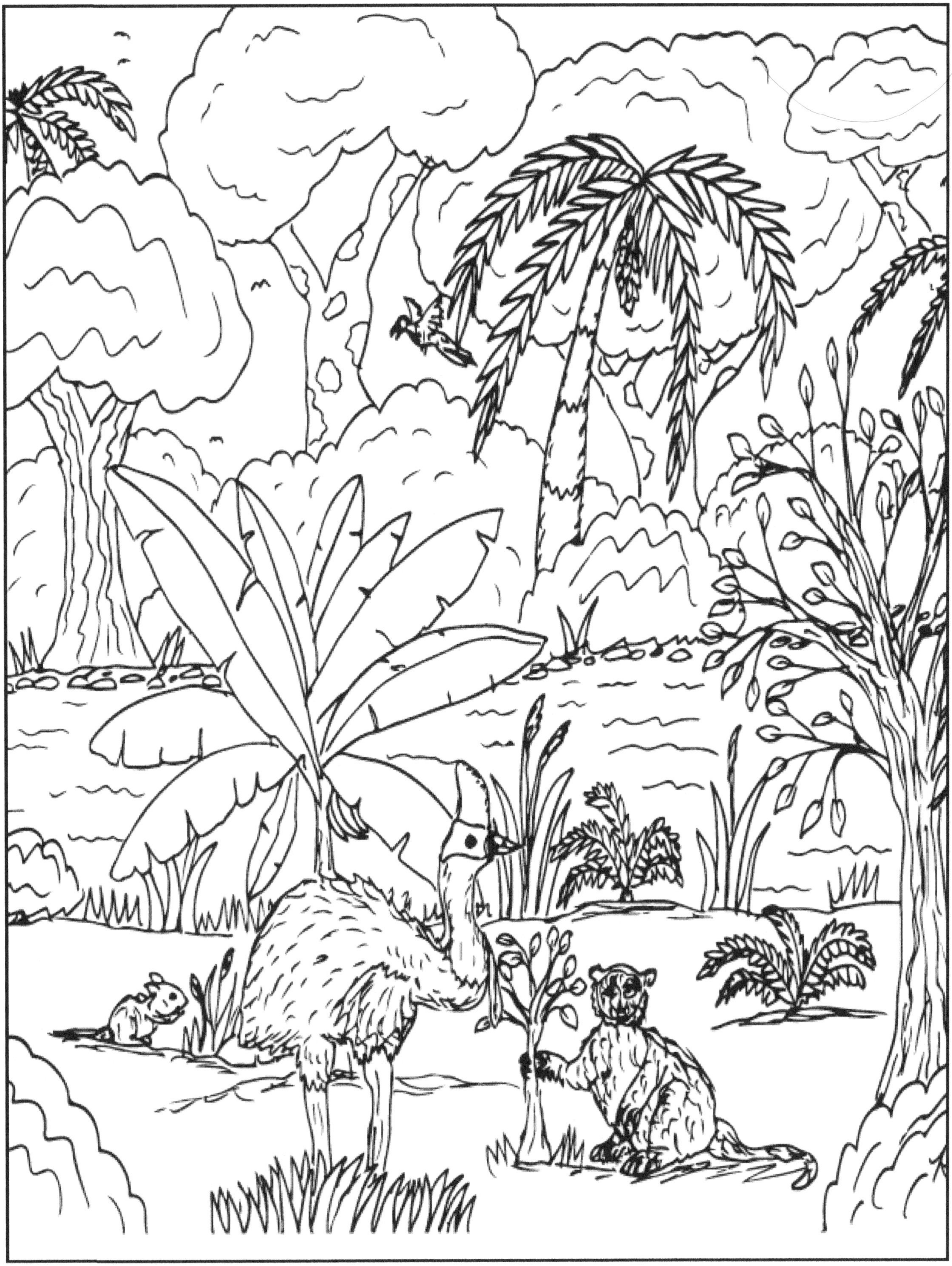

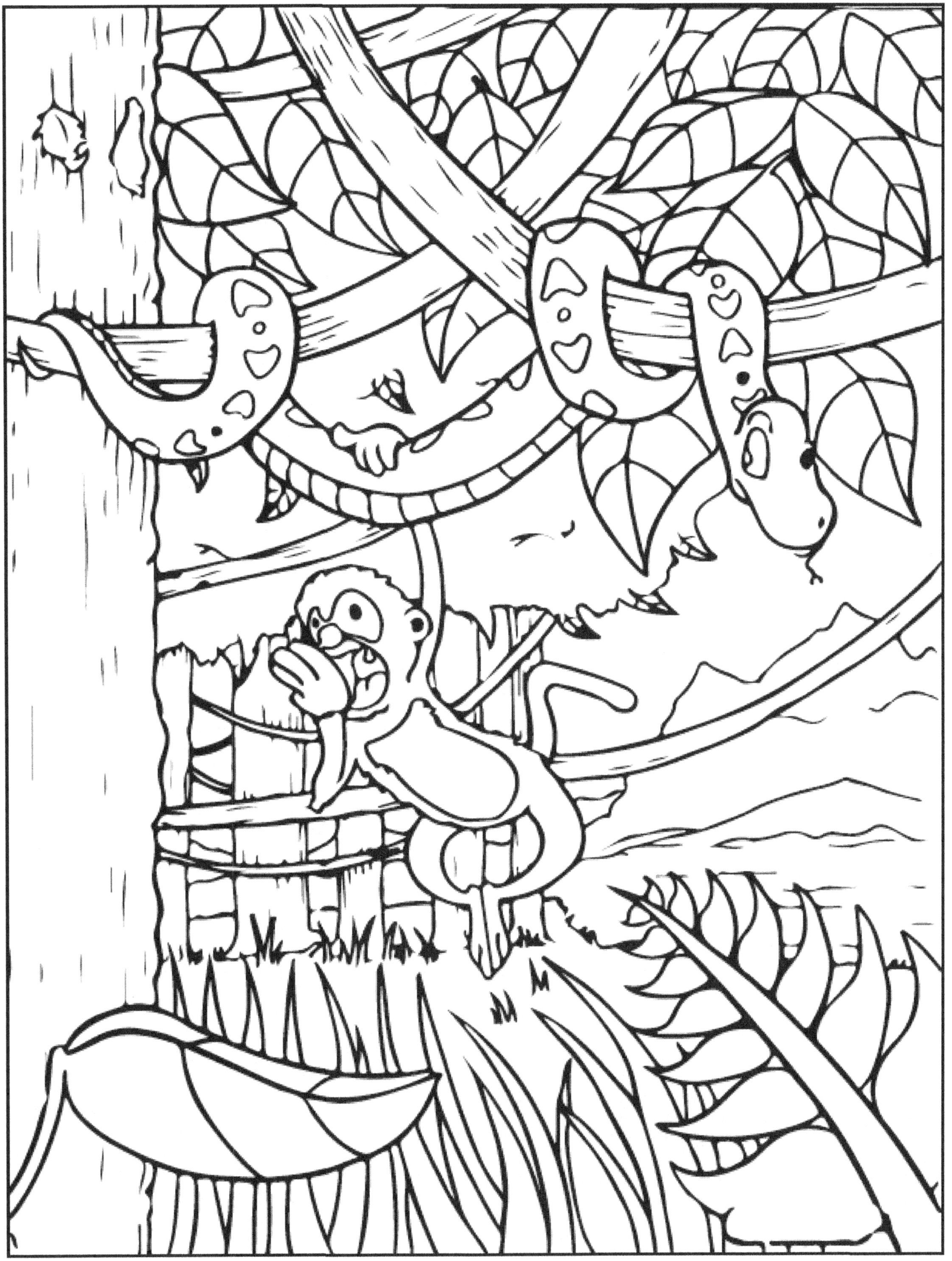

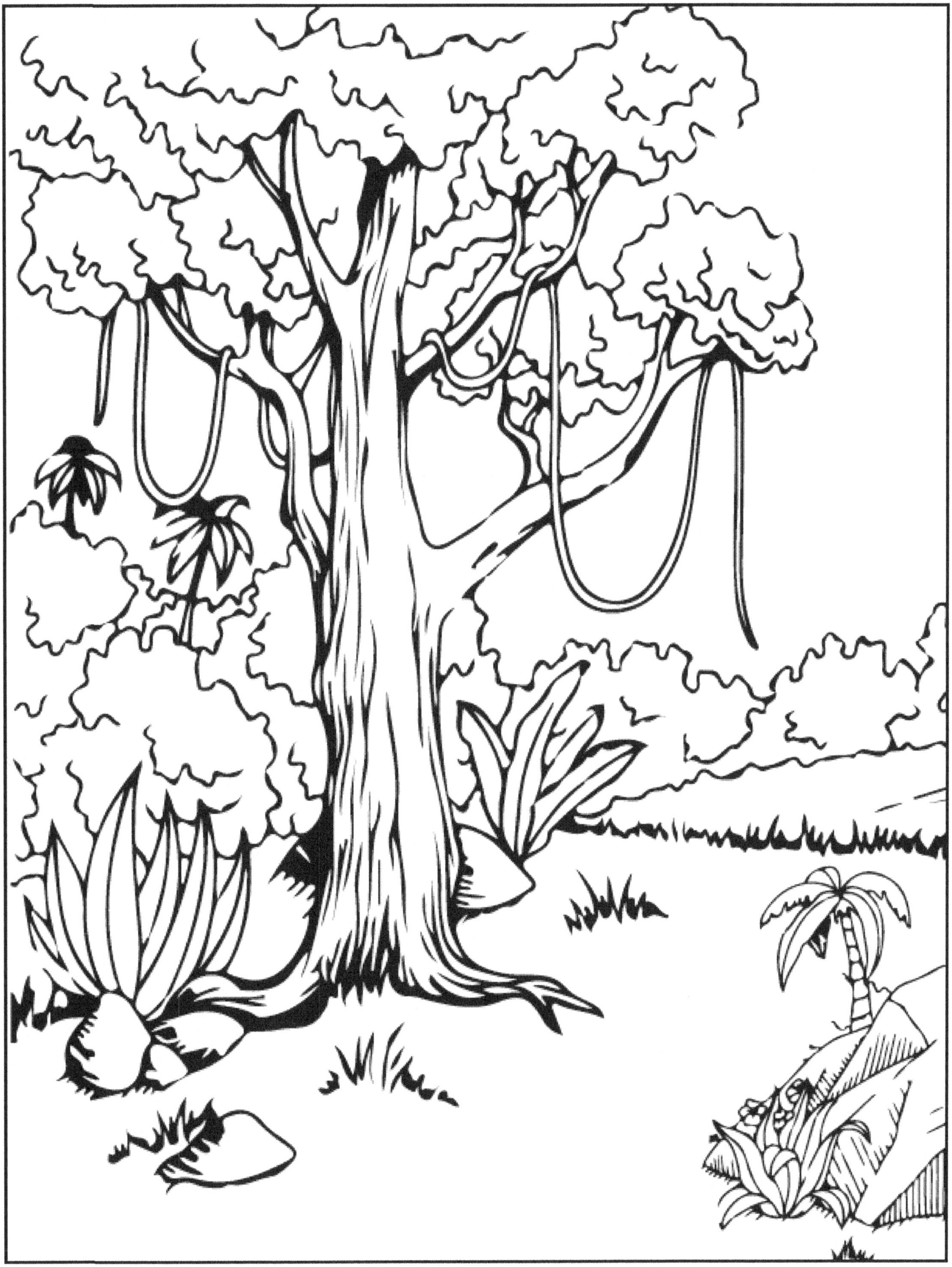

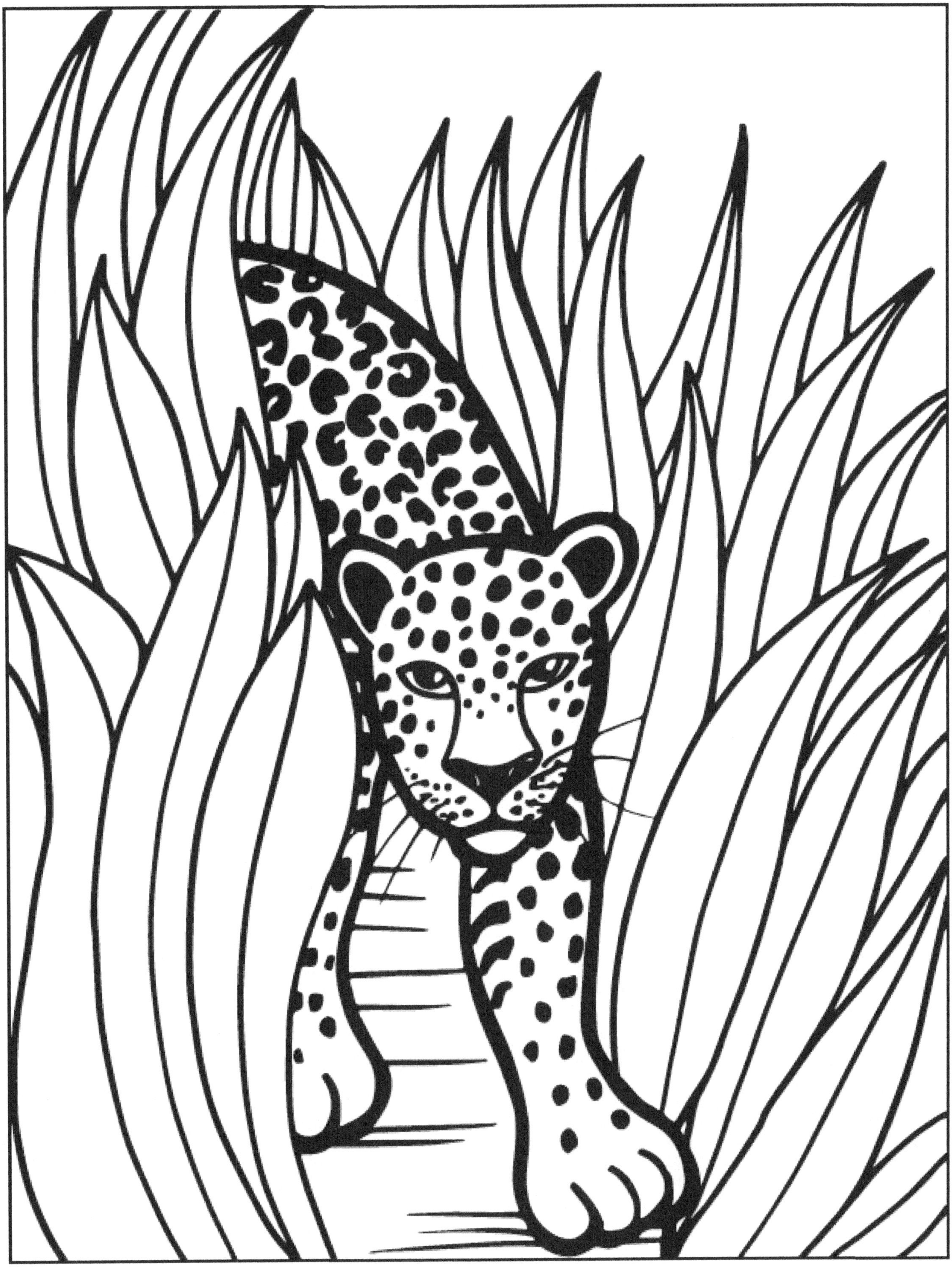

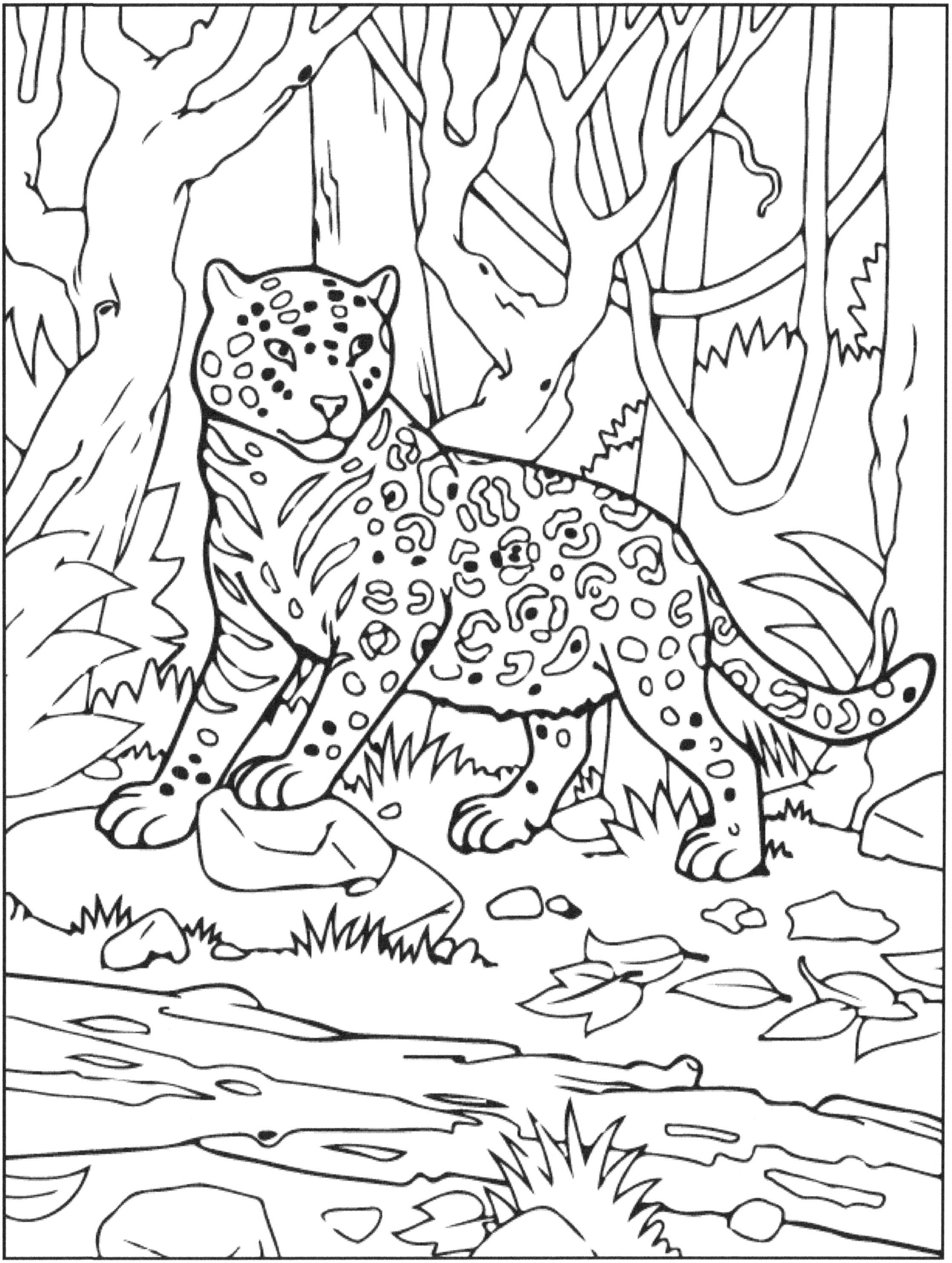

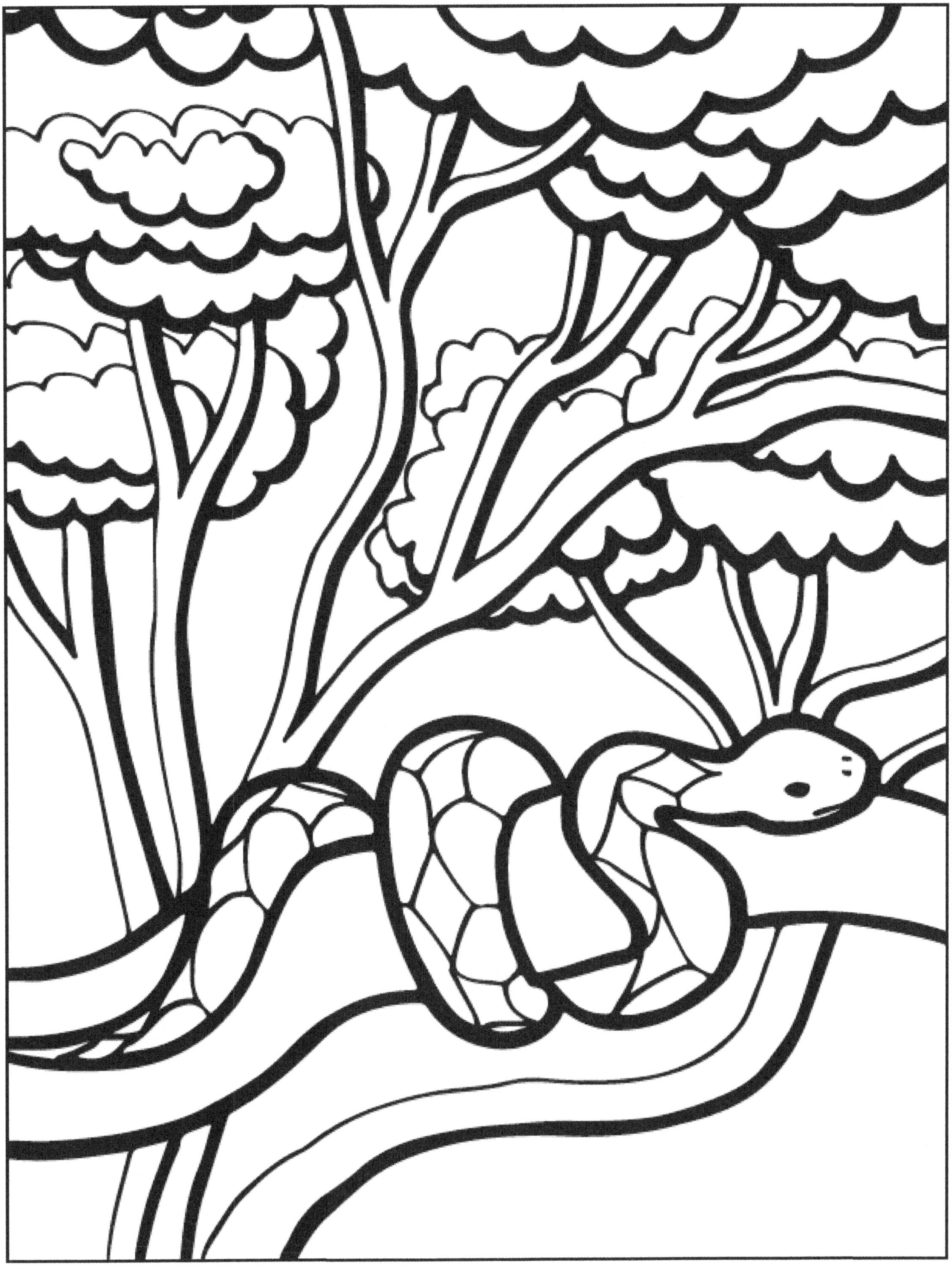

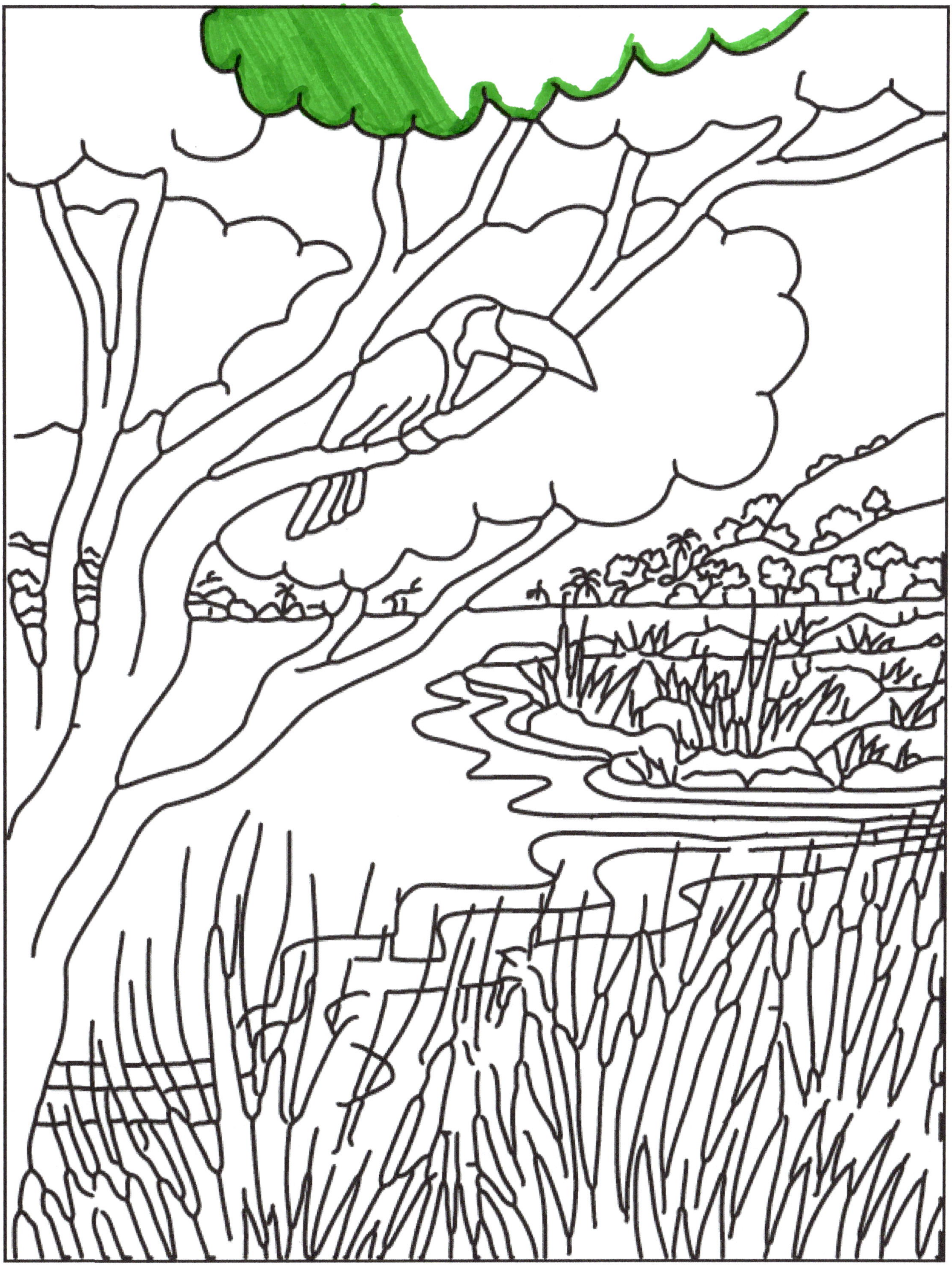

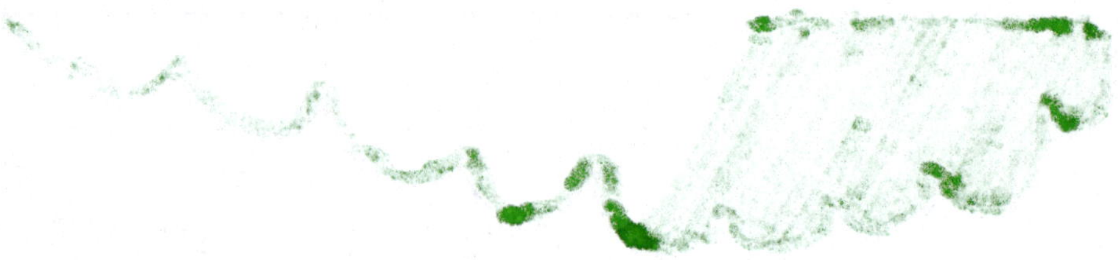

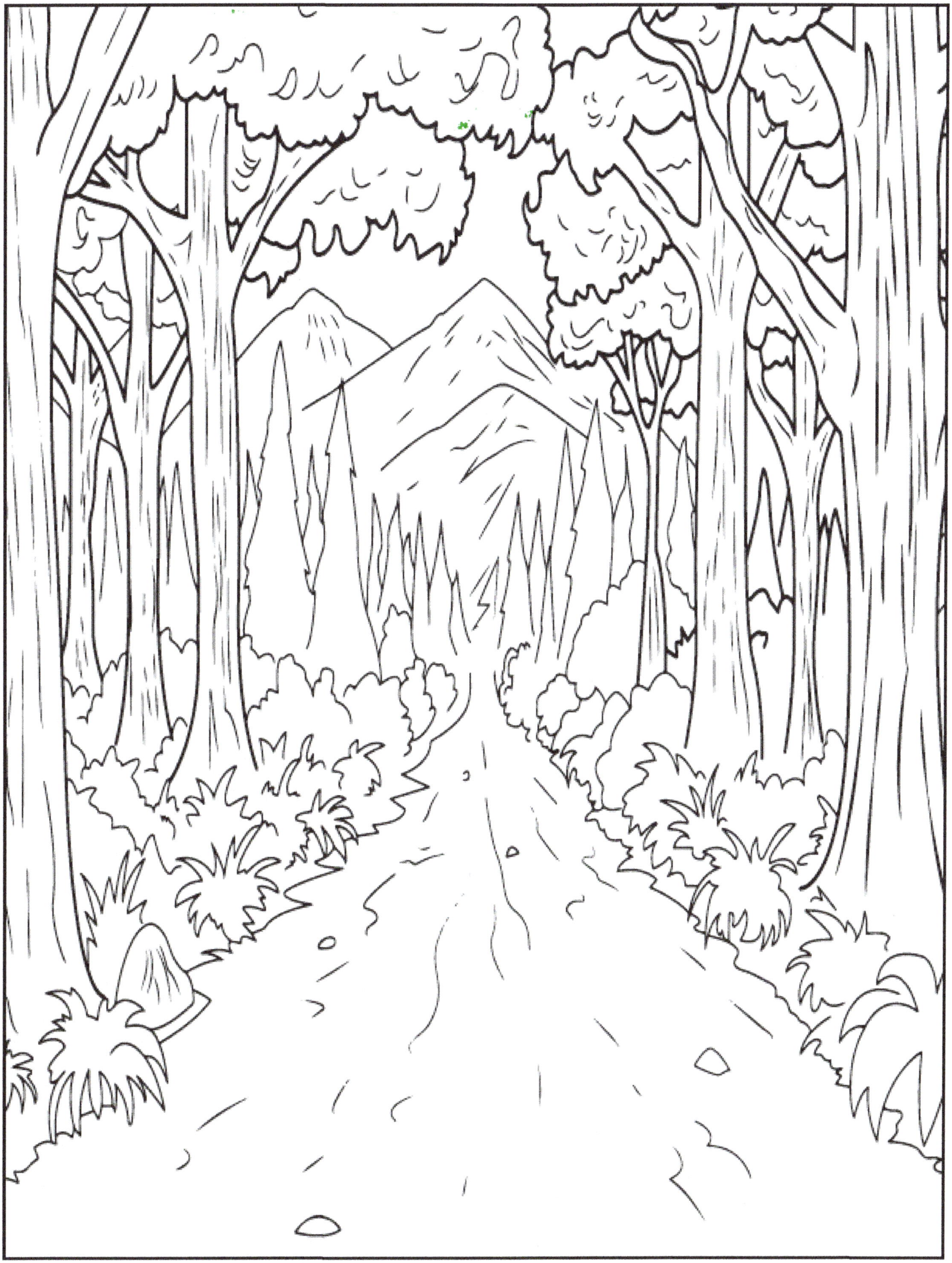

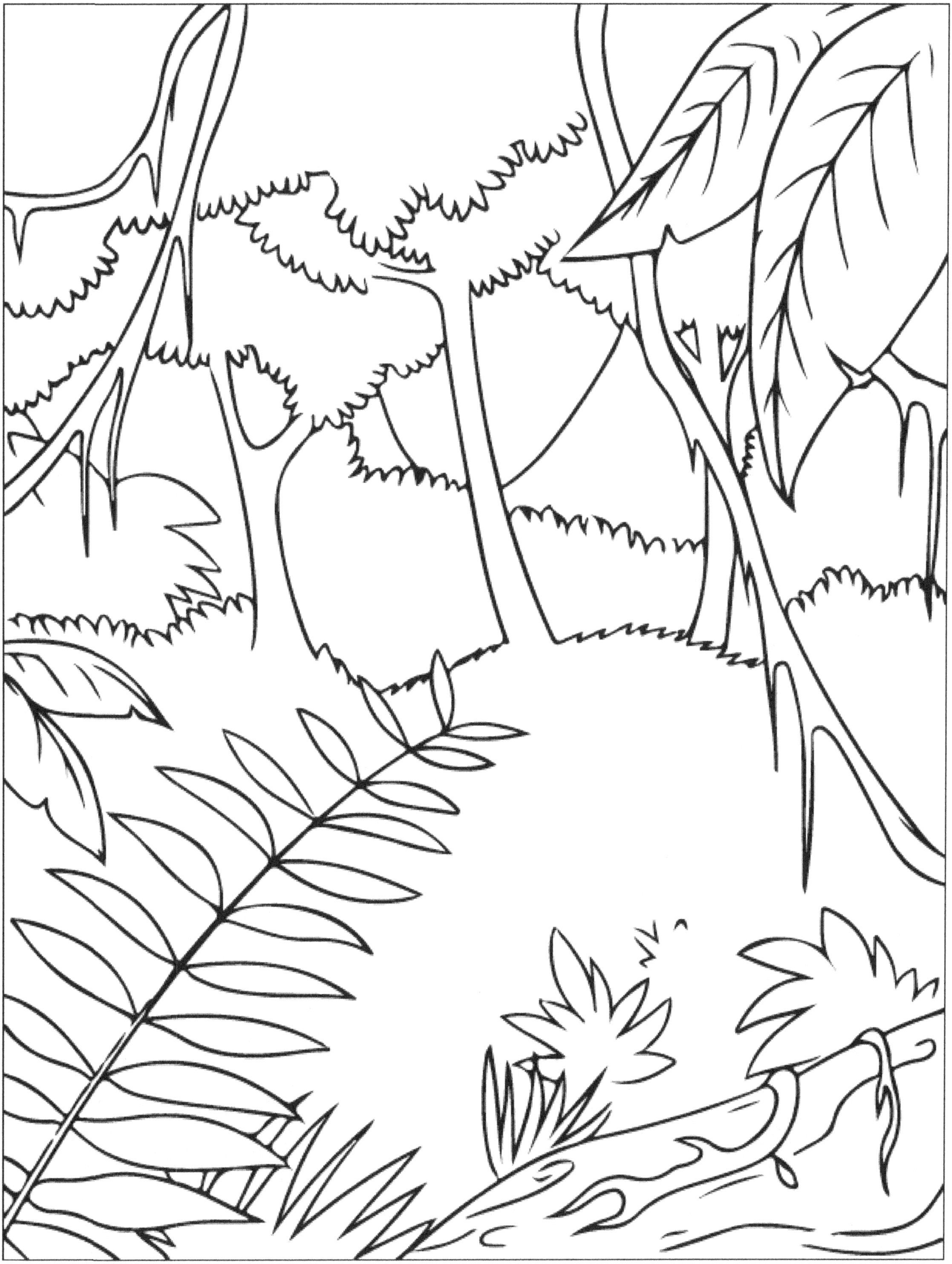

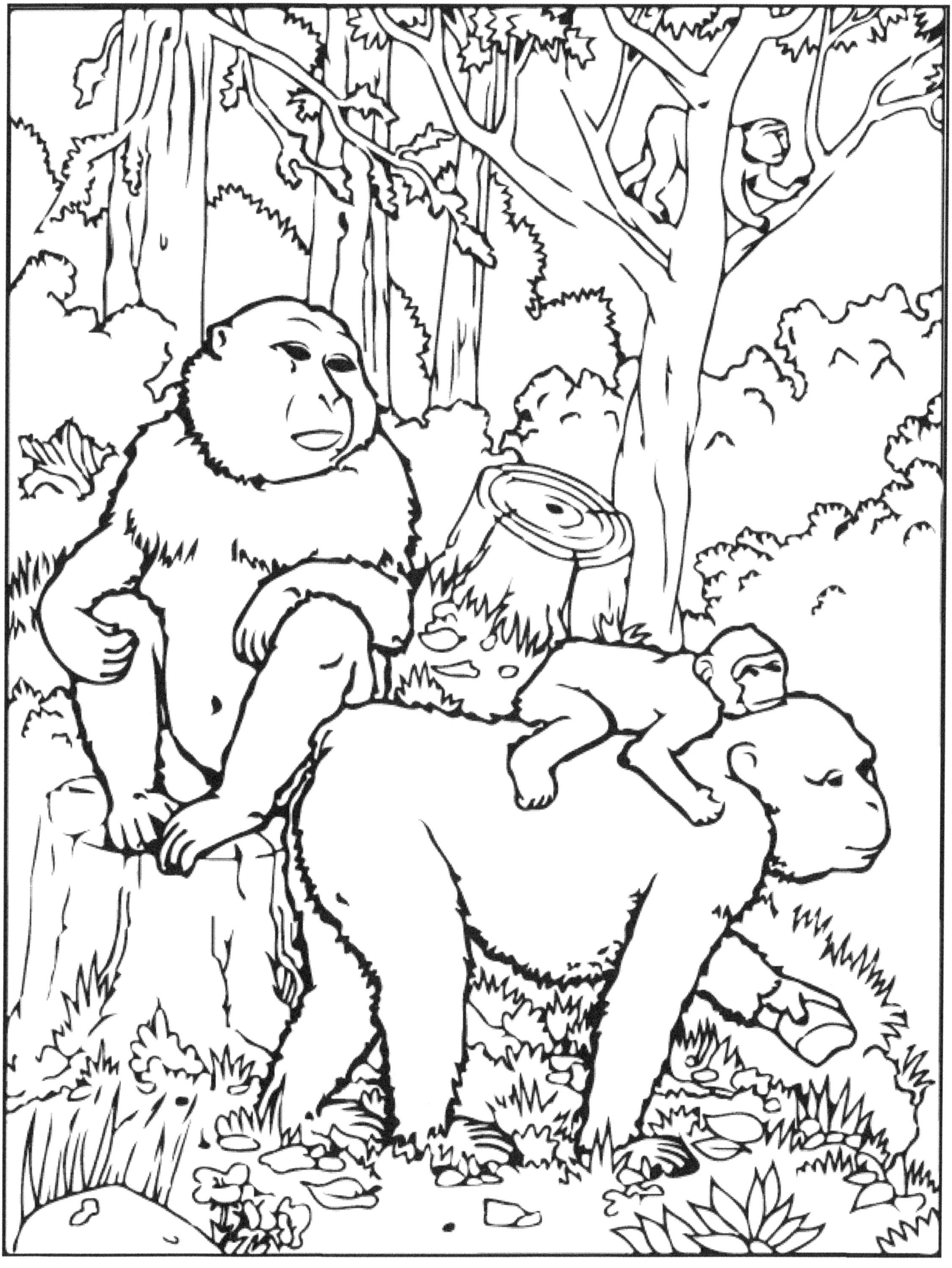

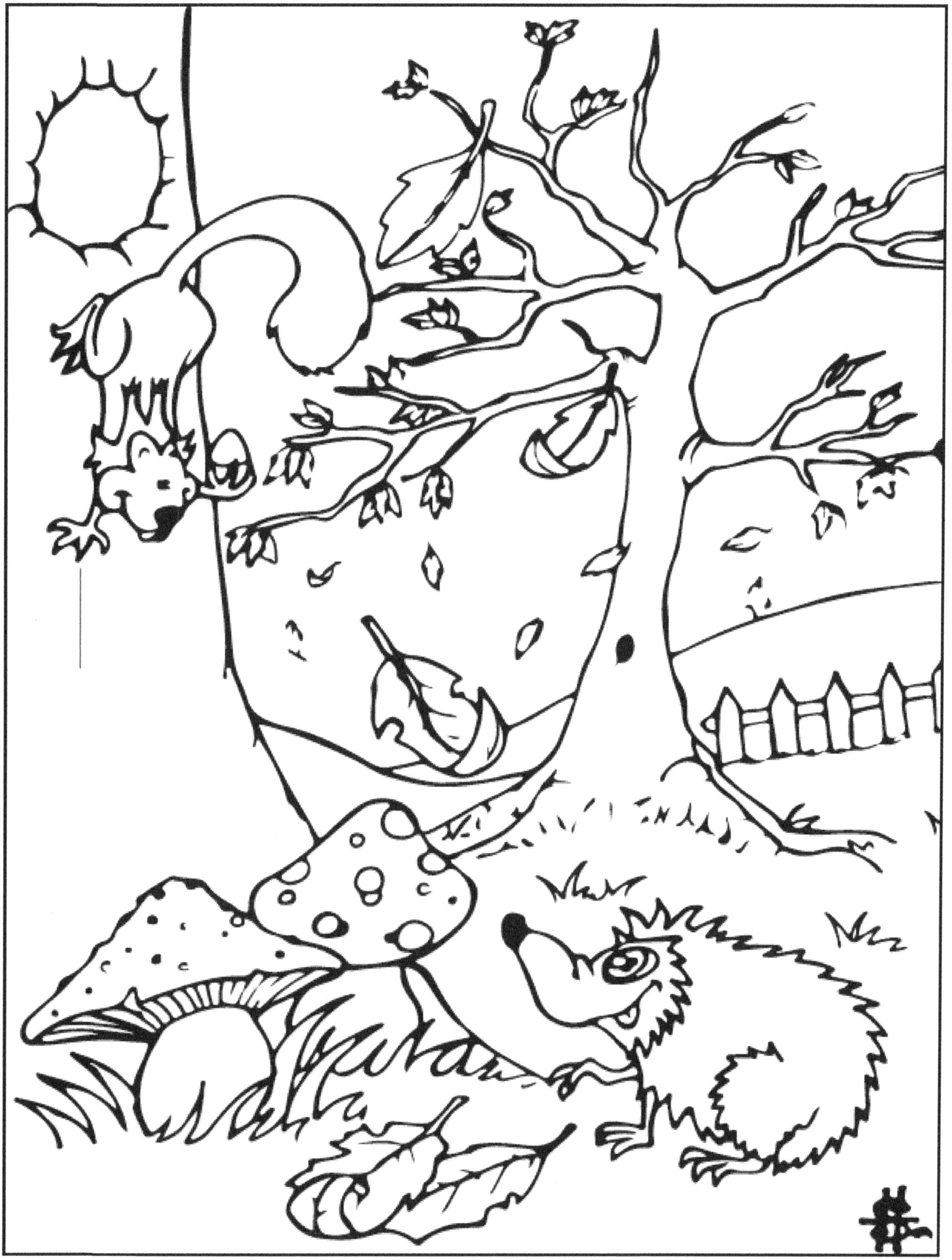

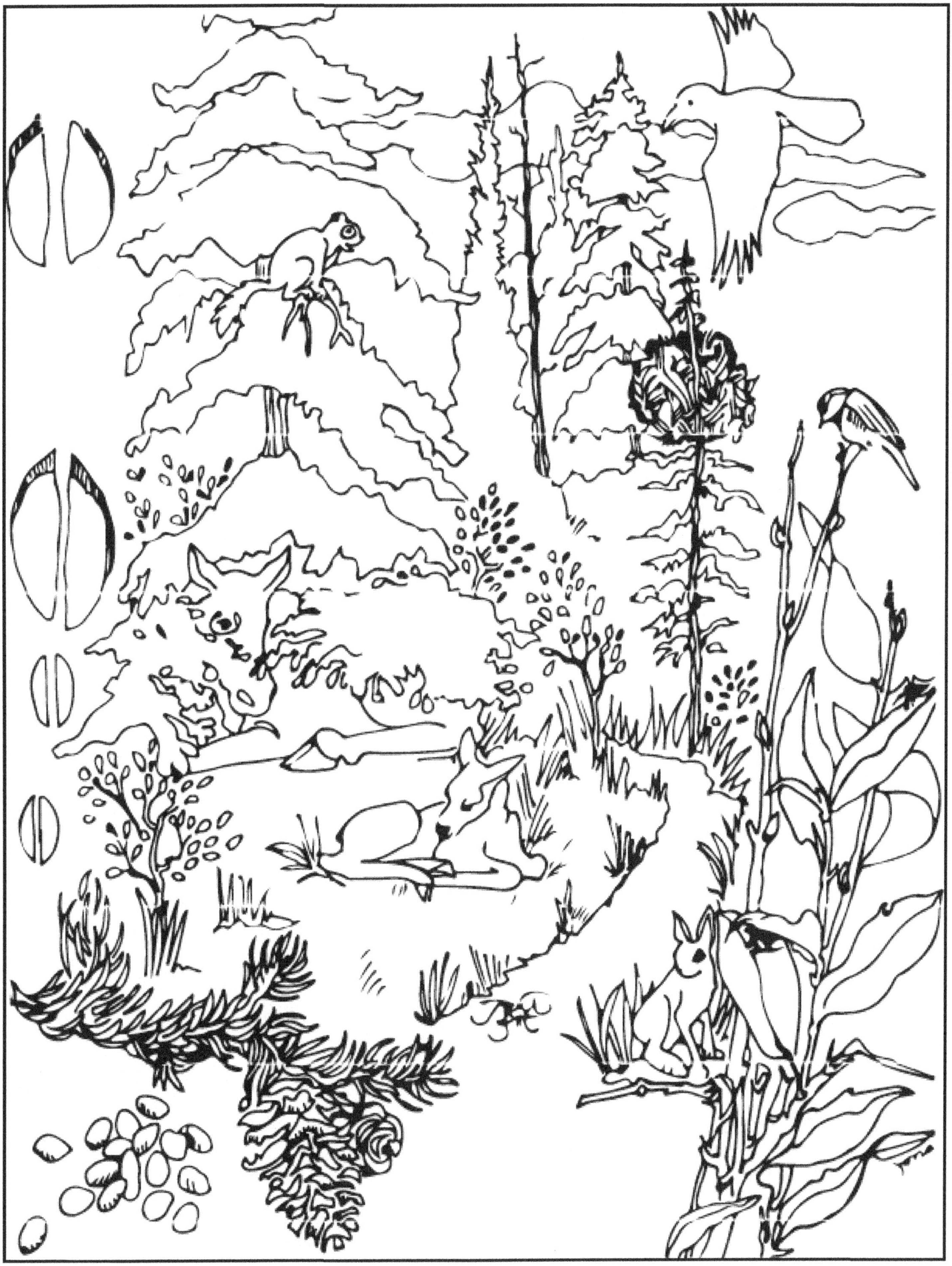

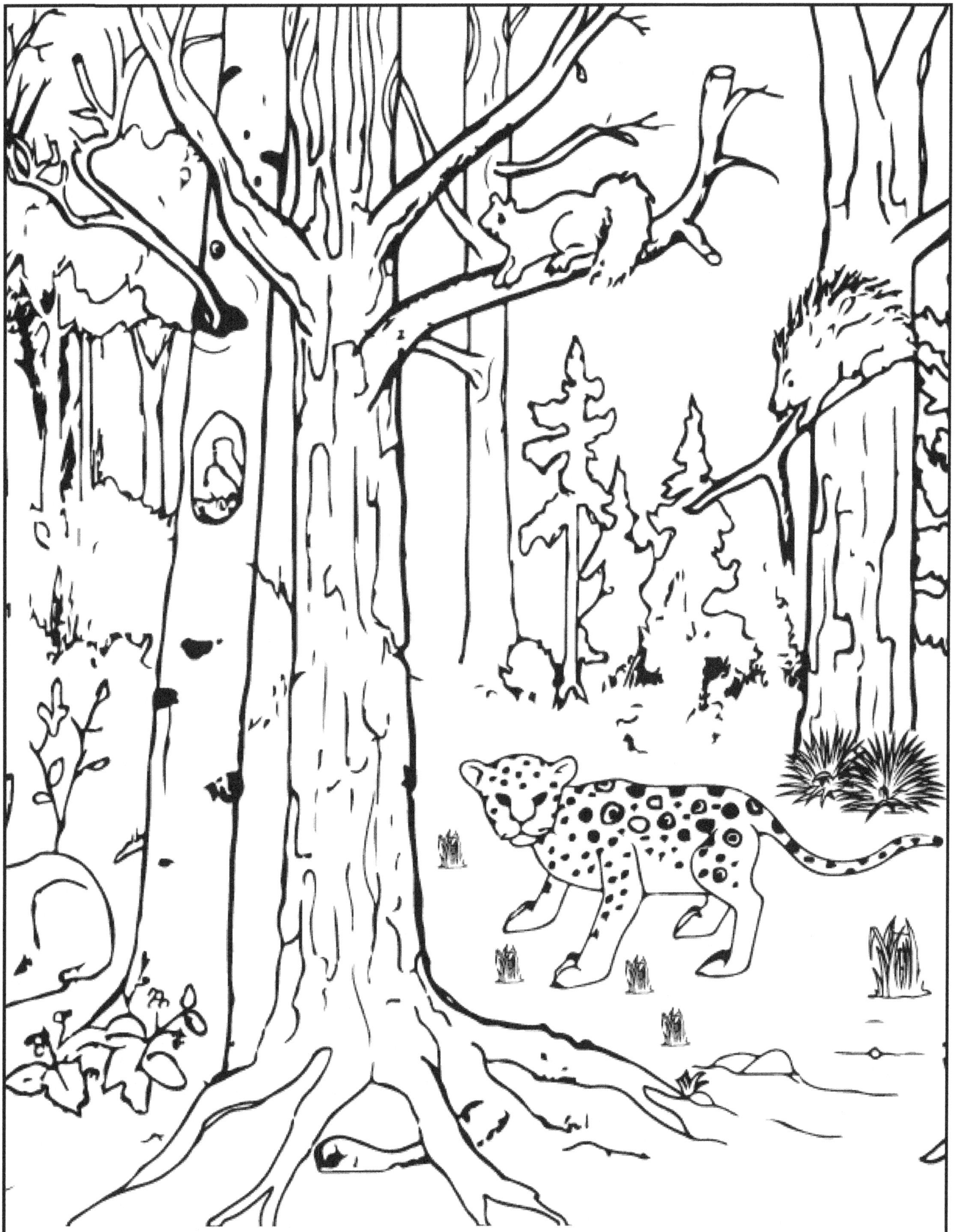

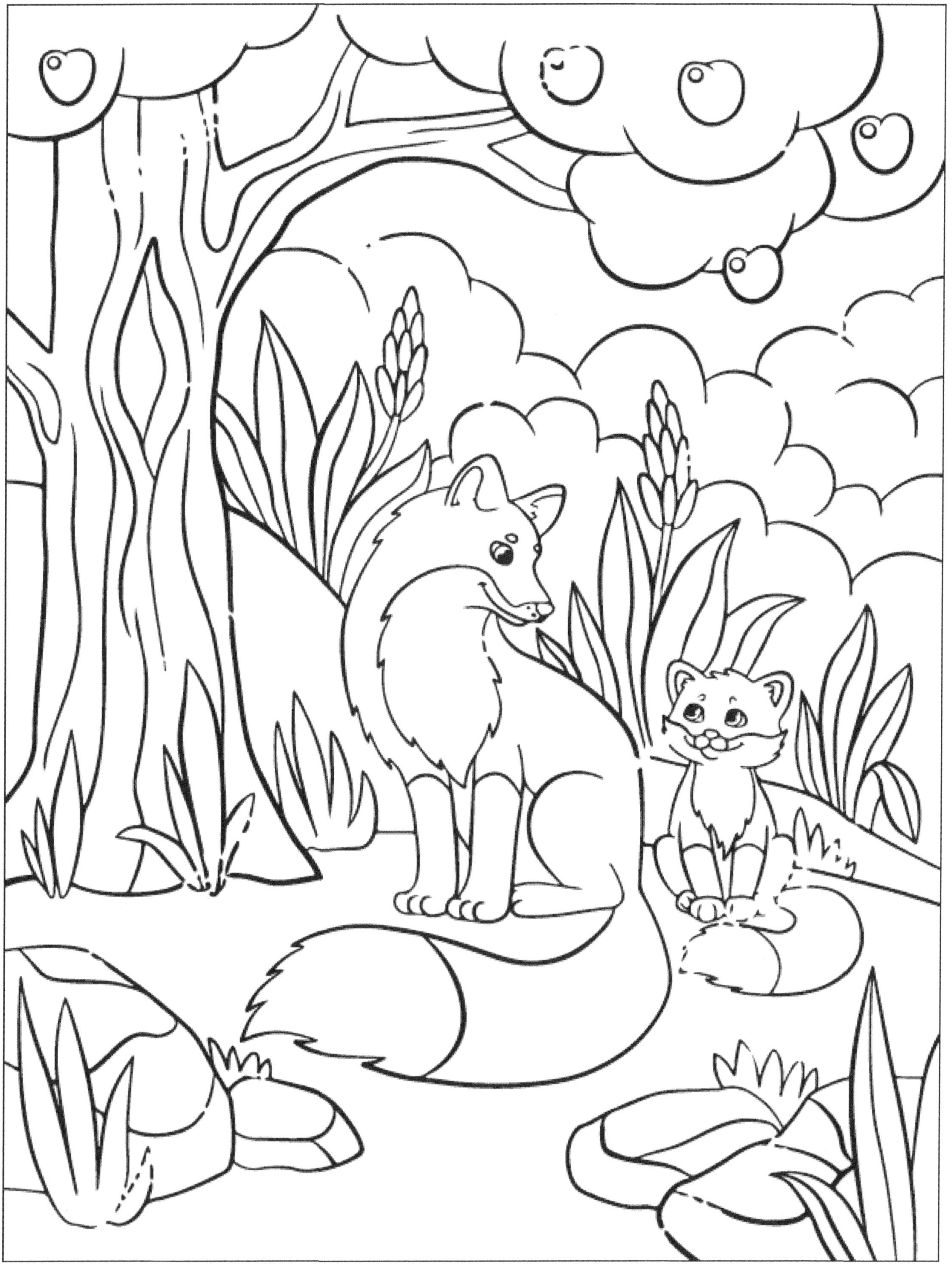

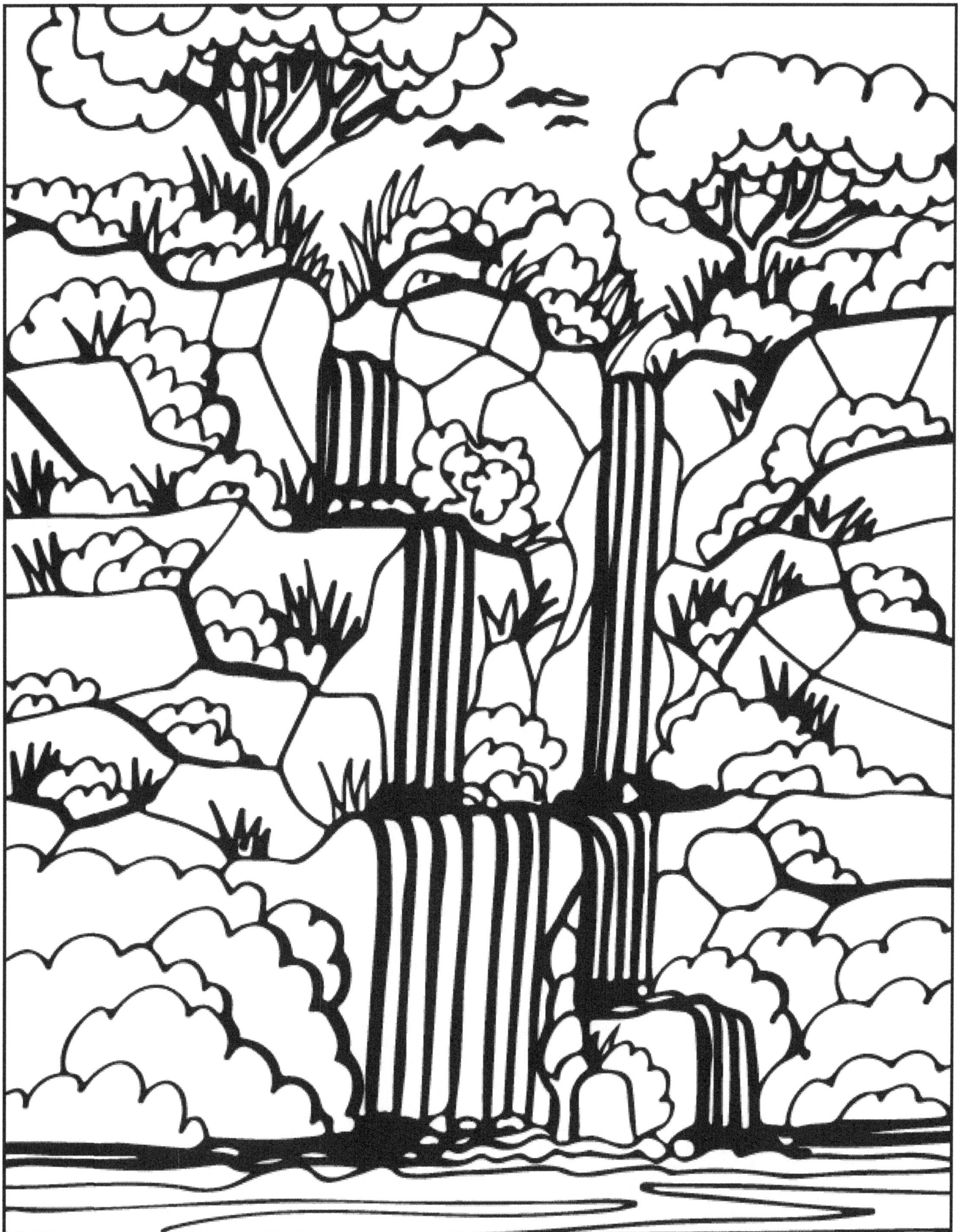

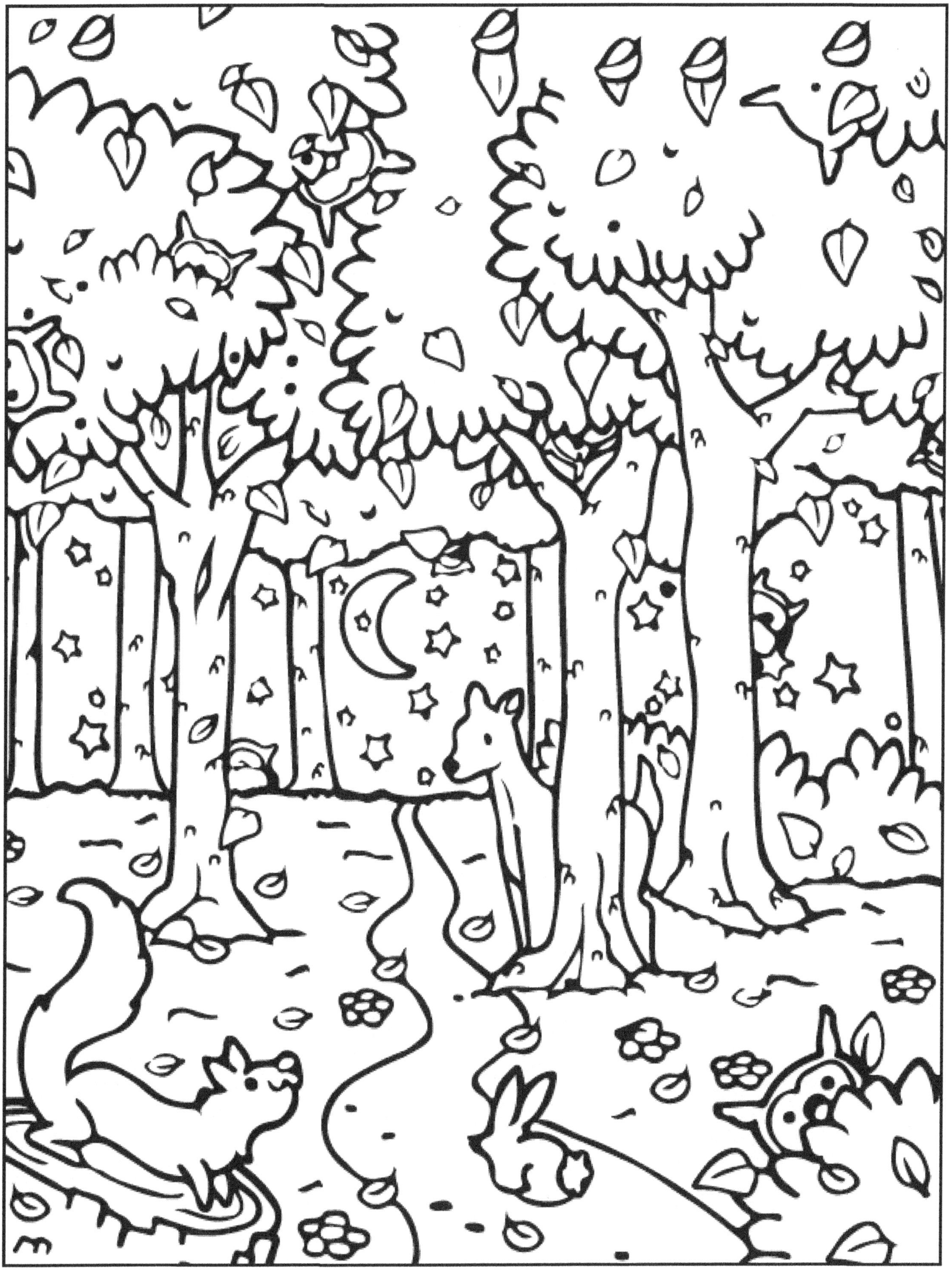

# Save The Rainforest

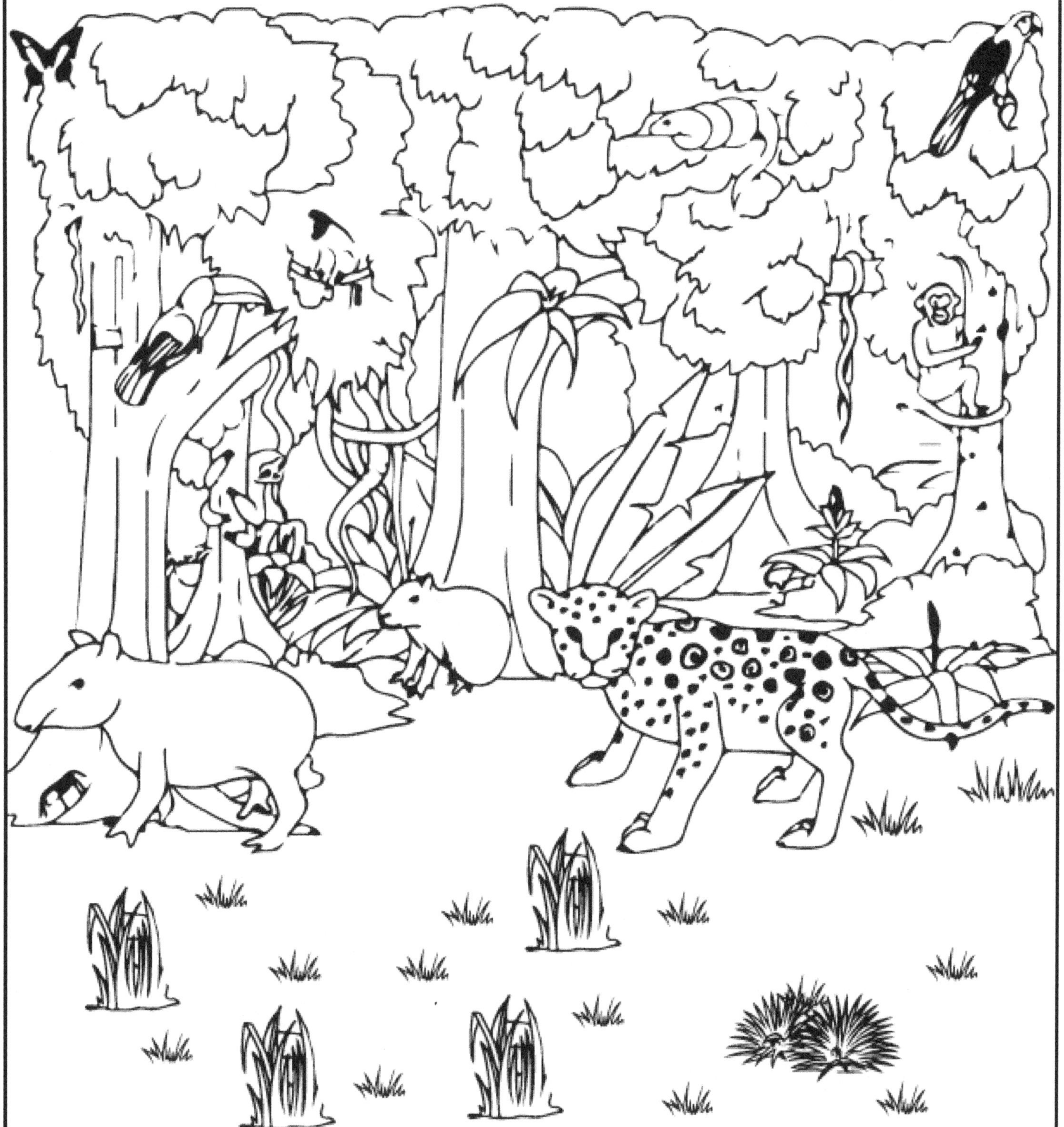

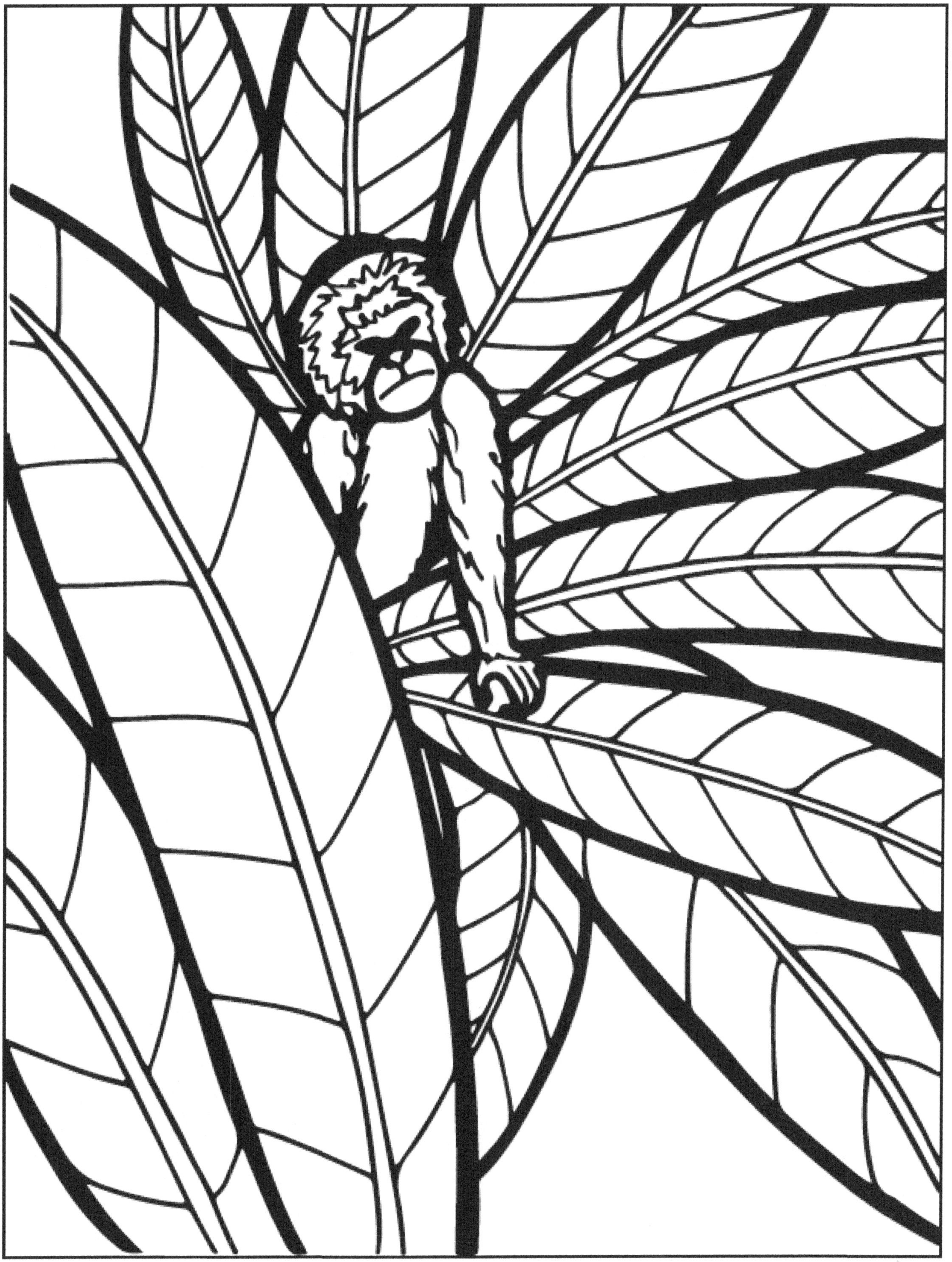

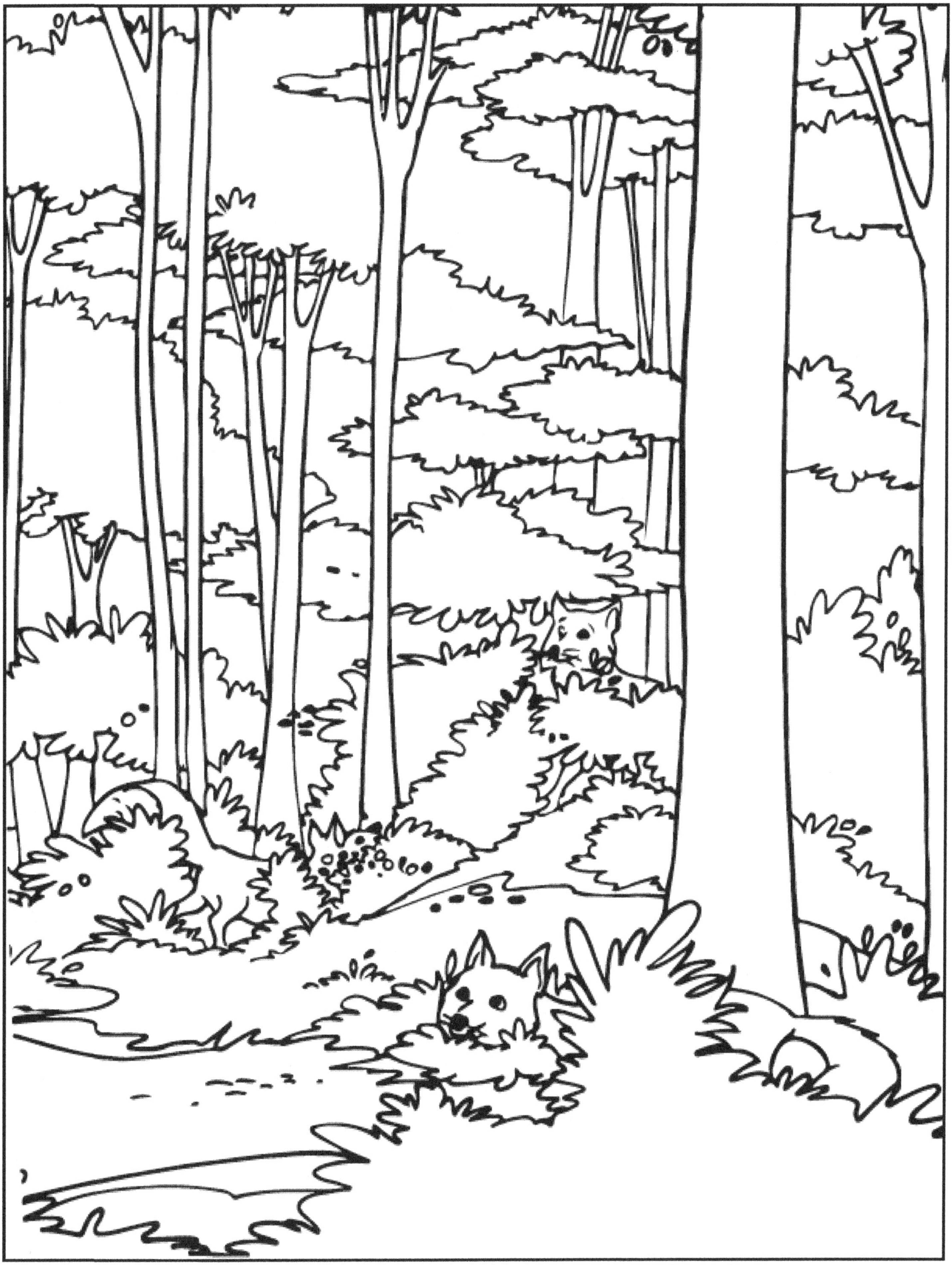

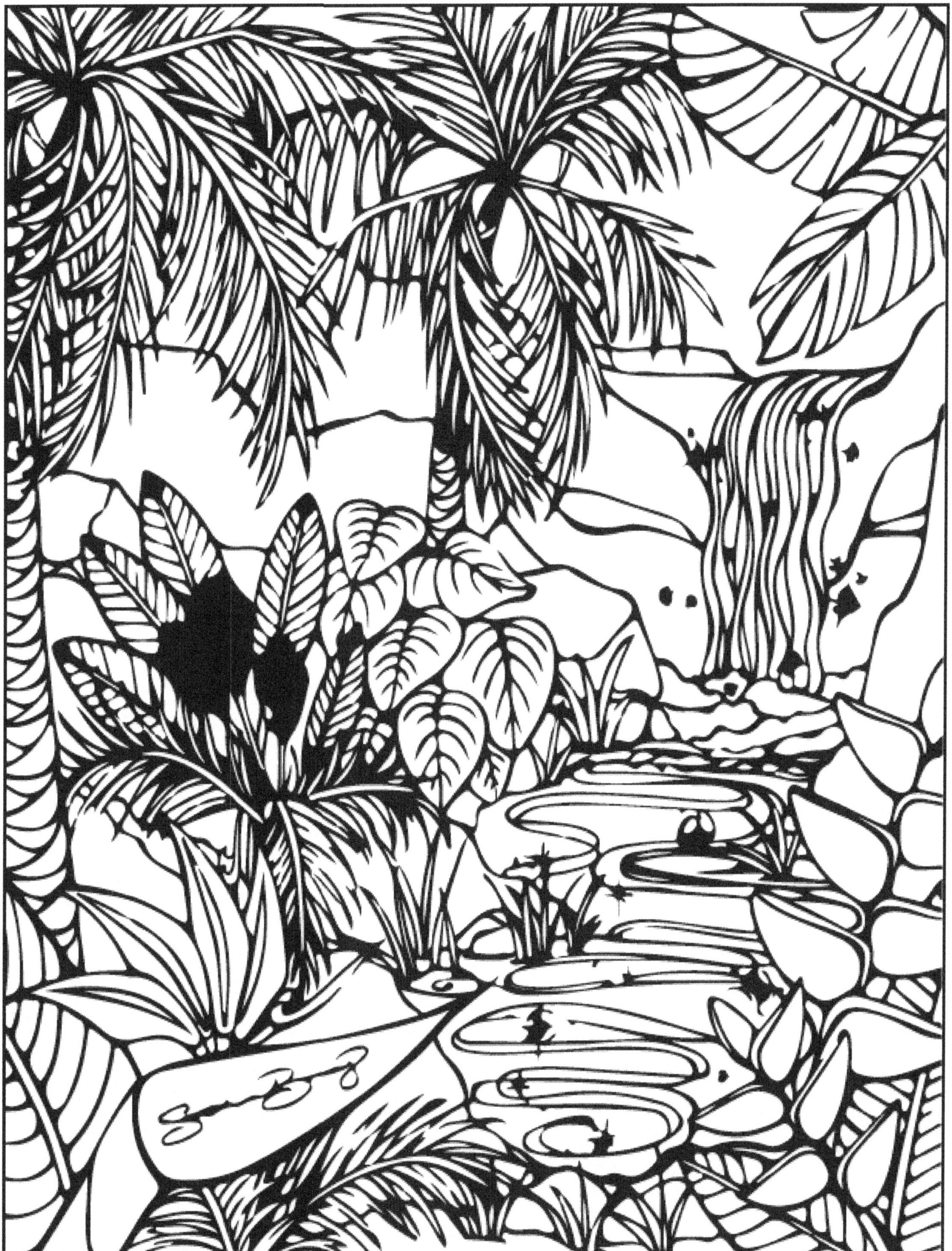

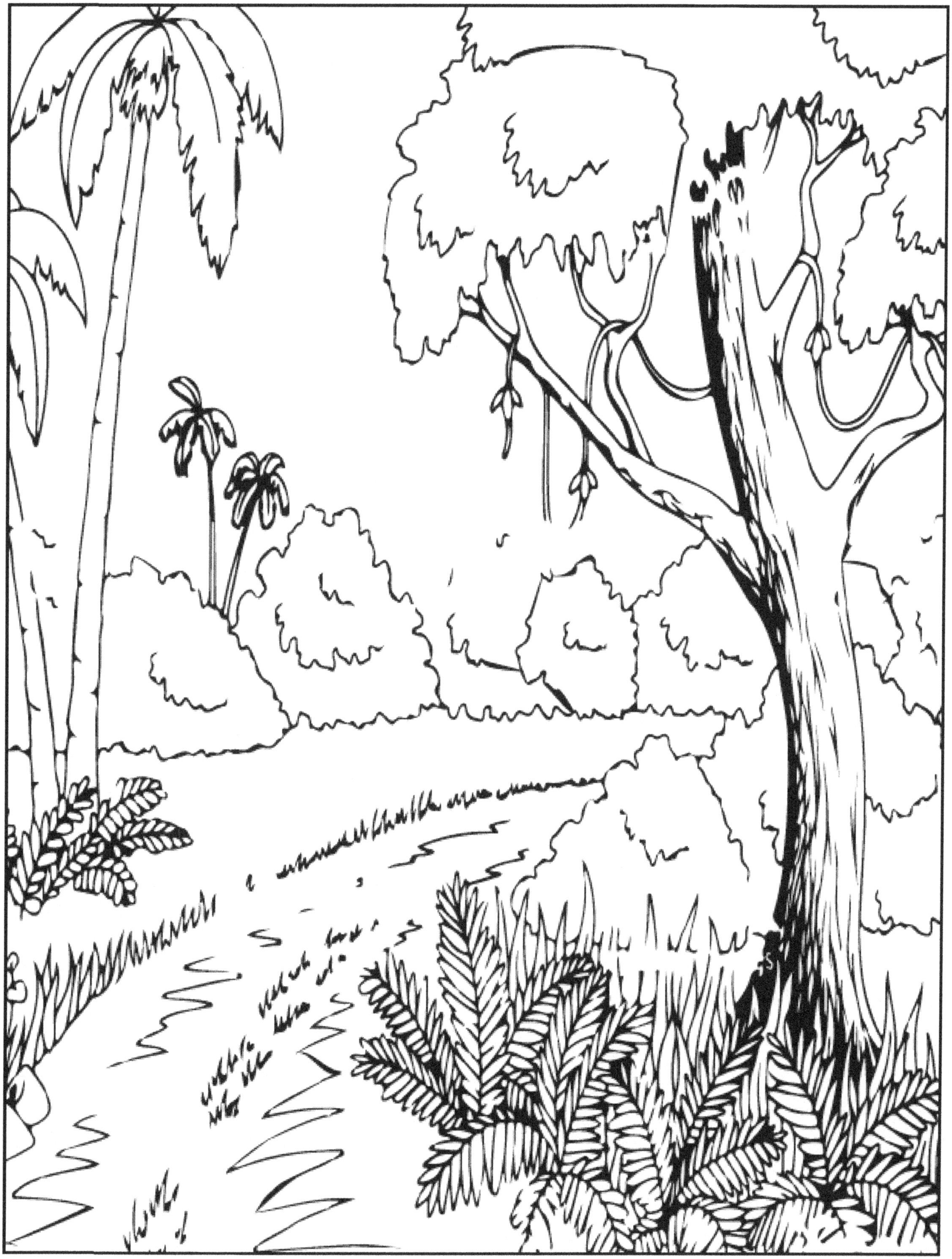

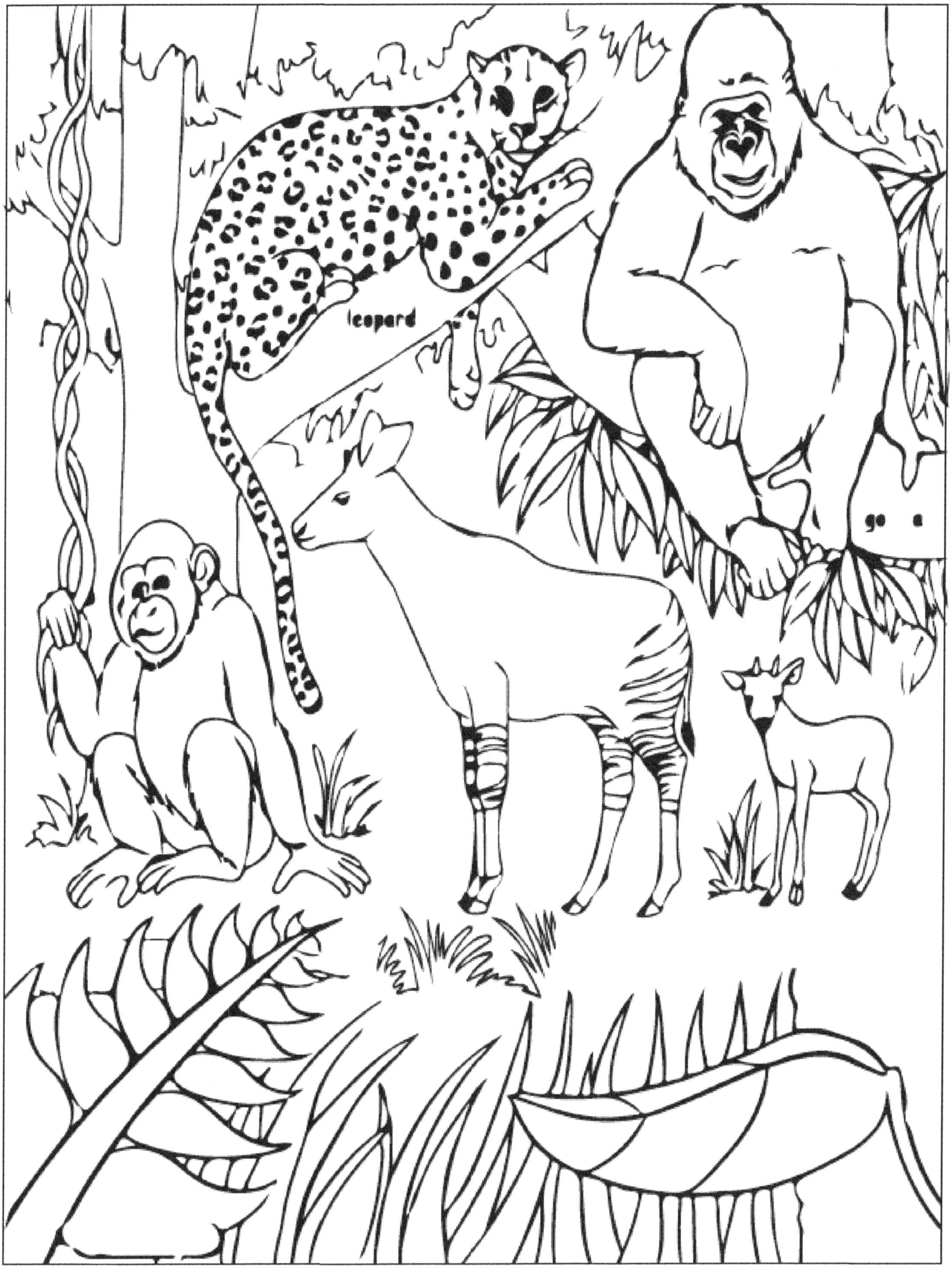
leopard
go a

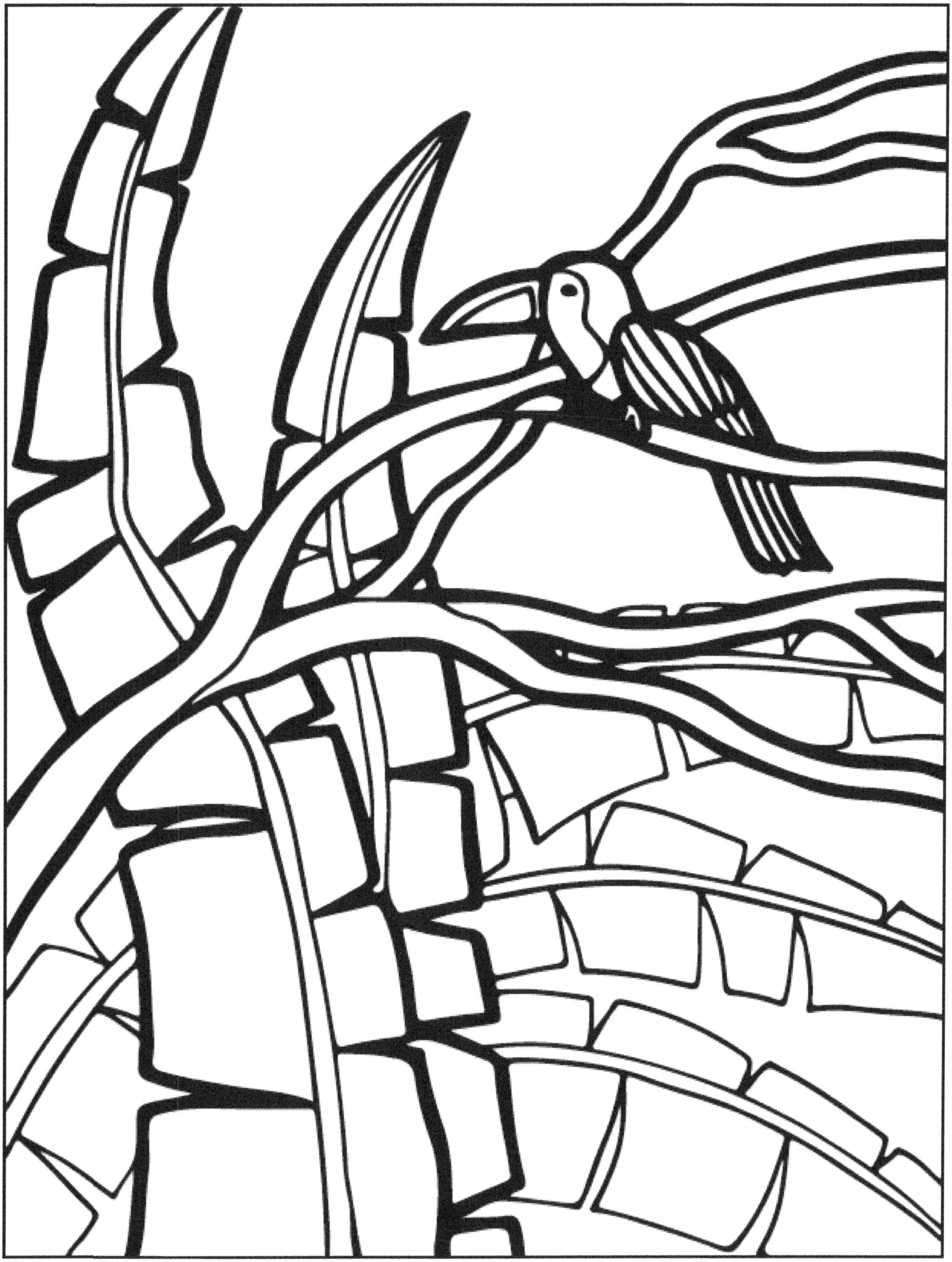

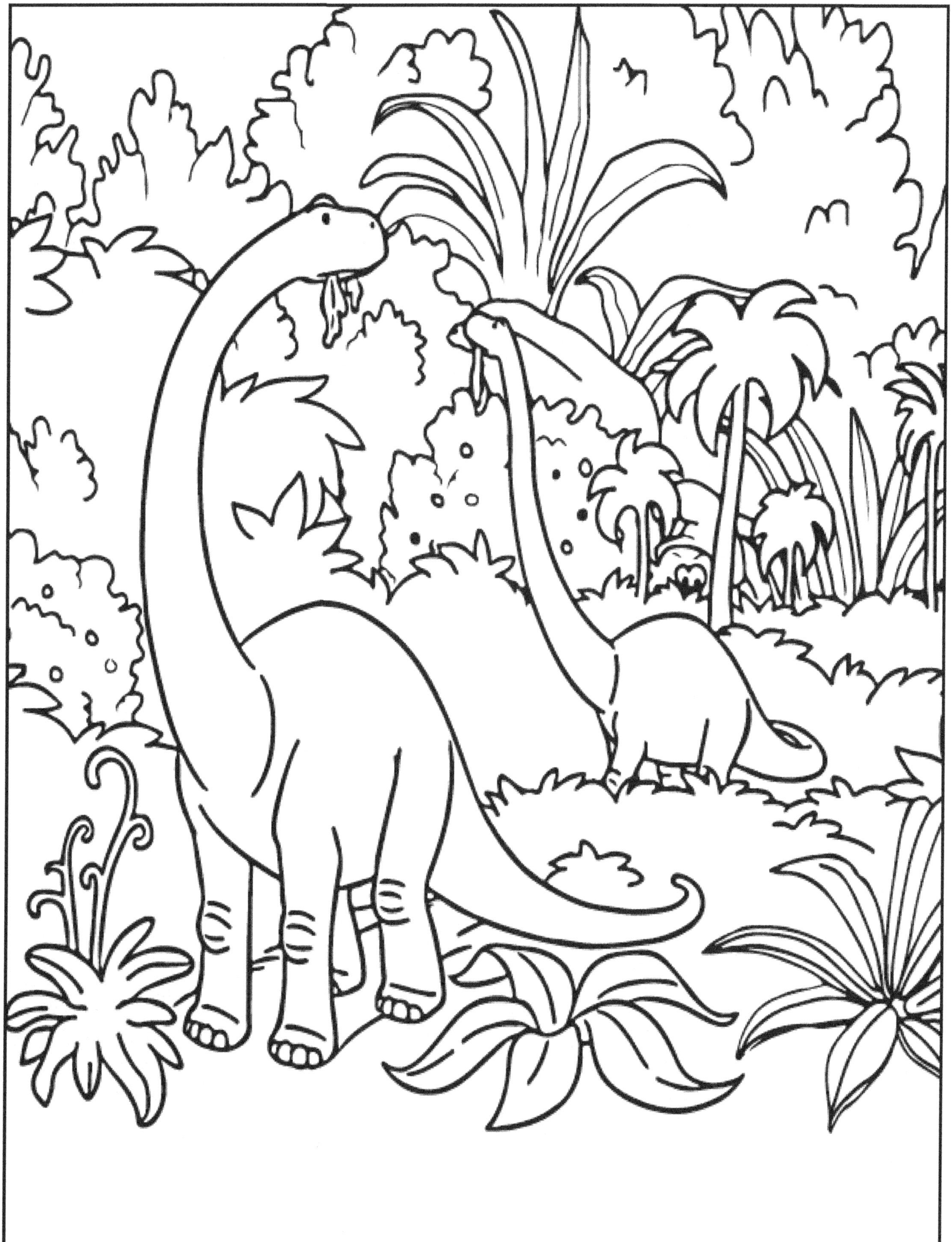

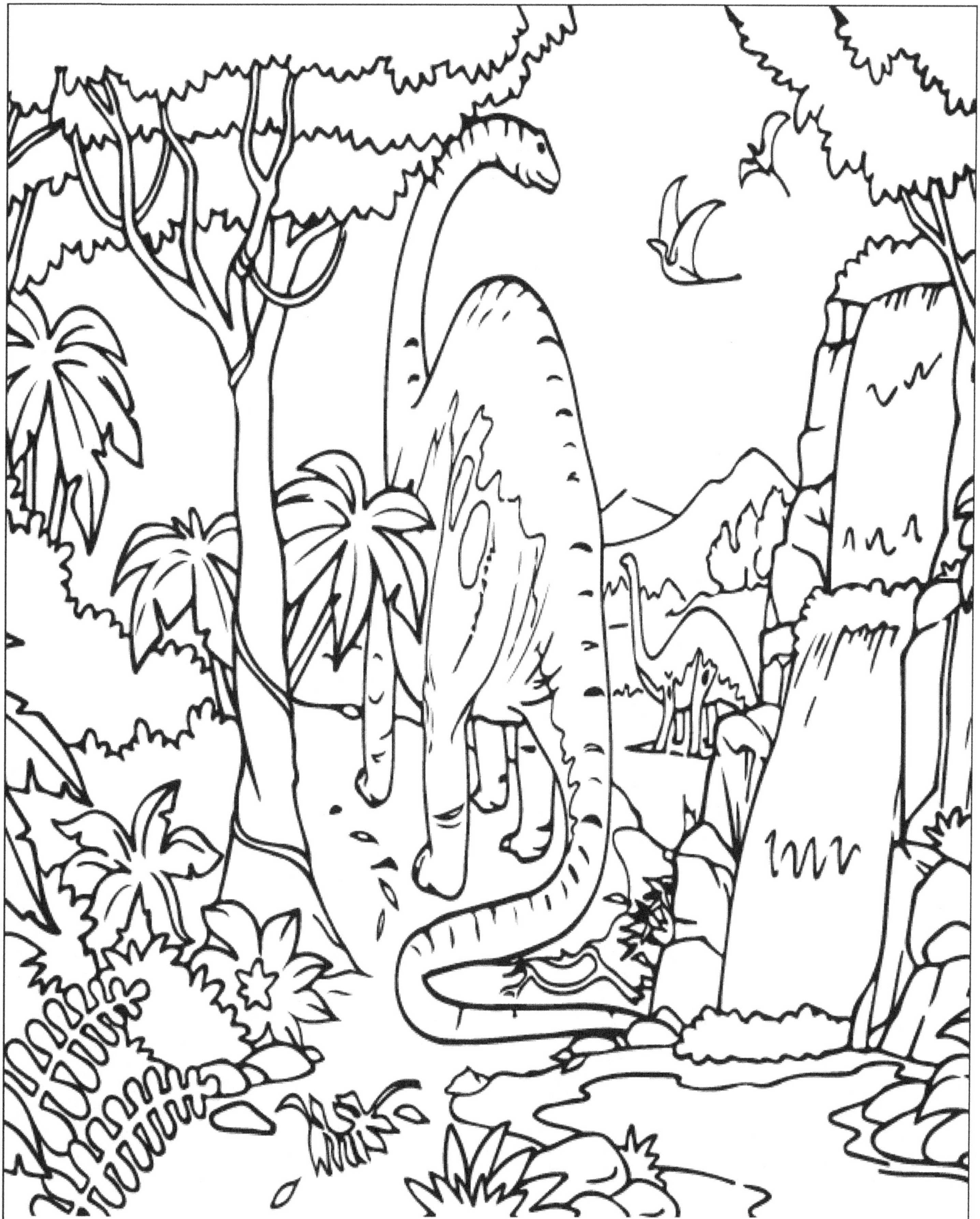

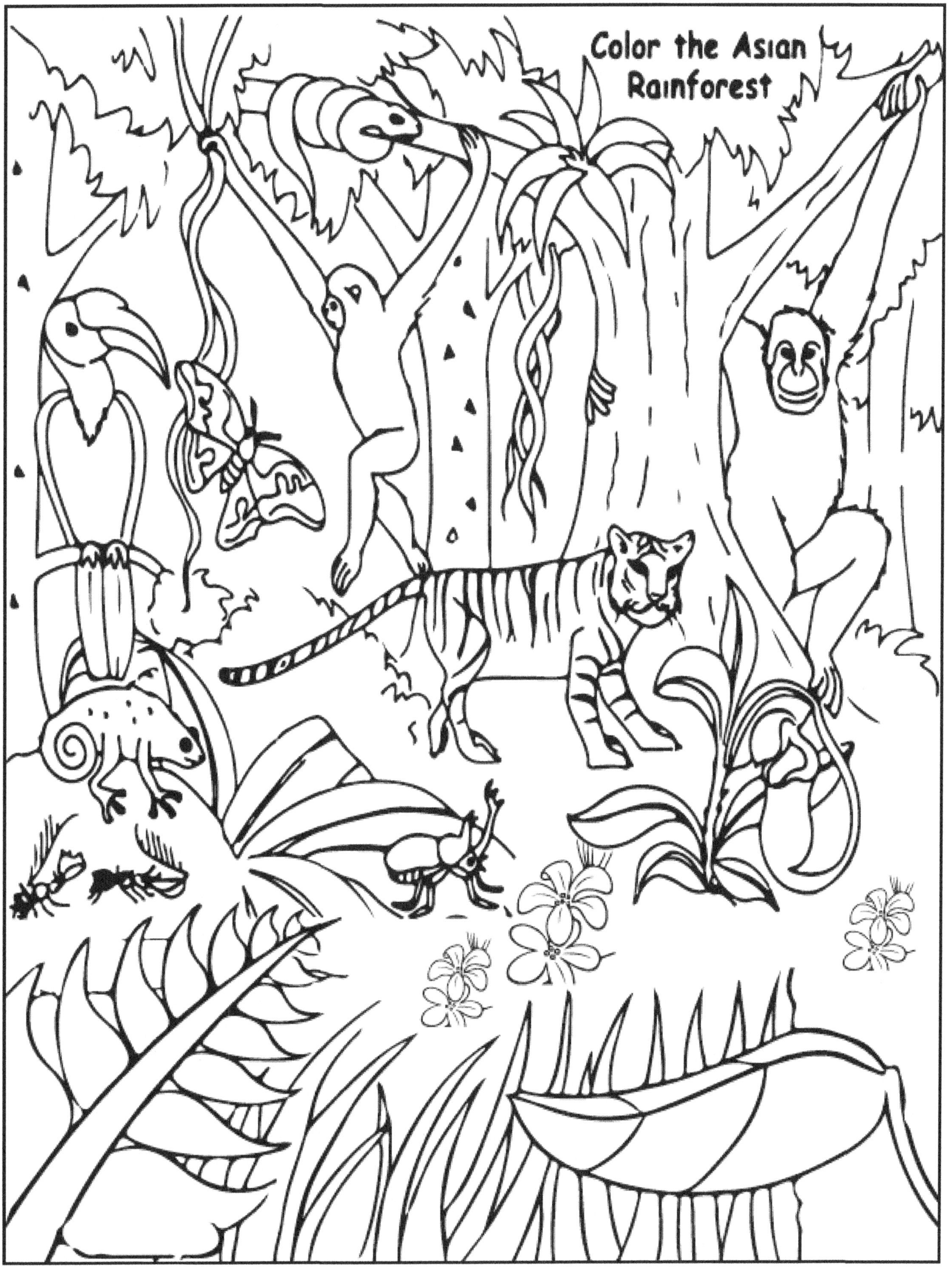
Color the Asian
Rainforest

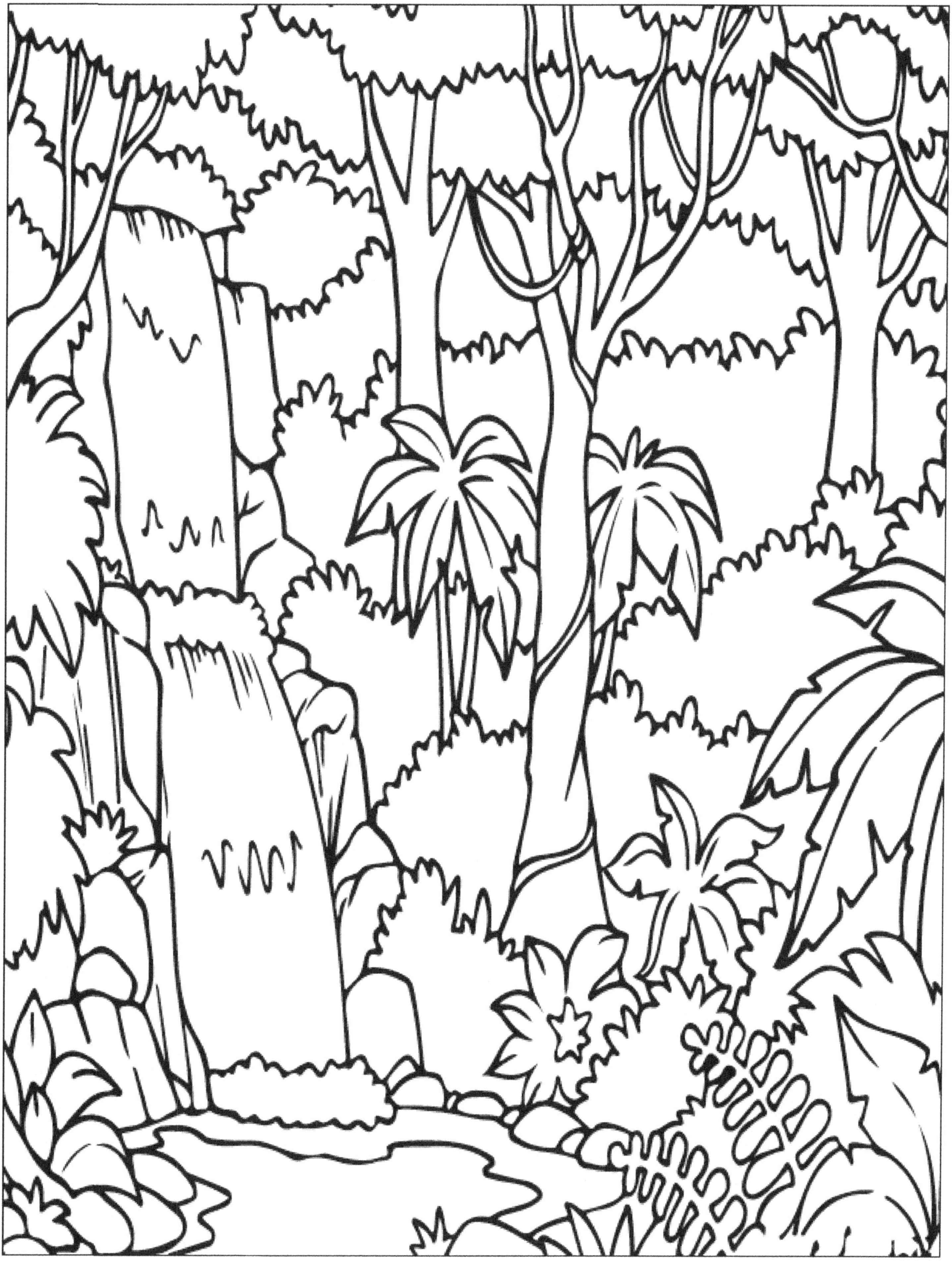

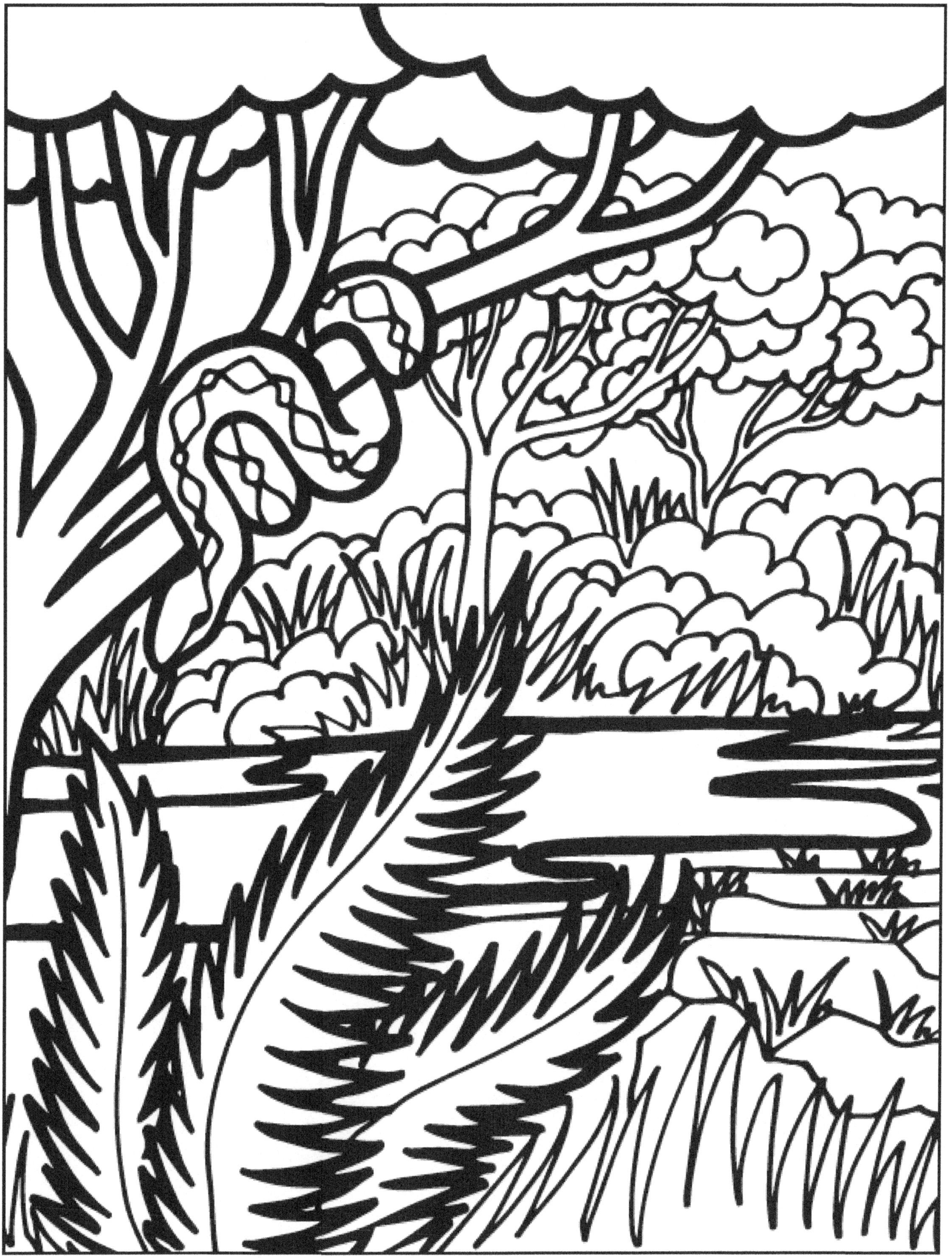

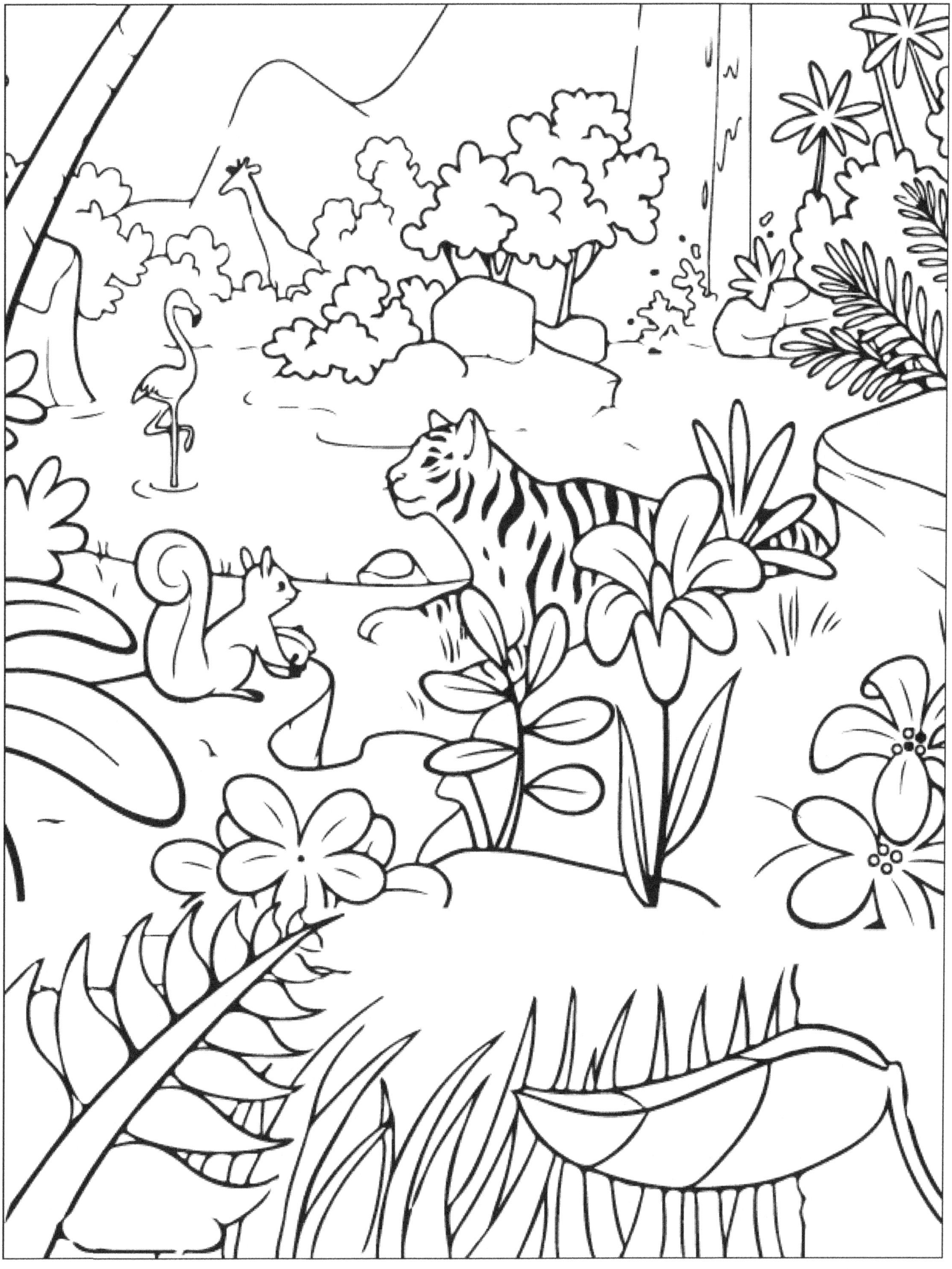

Made in the USA
Monee, IL
12 March 2022

92503654R00046